Workbook

P9-DUA-243

³Workplace Plus

Living and Working in English

Joan Saslow

Workbook by
Barbara R. Denman

Longman

Workplace Plus: Living and Working in English 3
Workbook

Copyright © 2003 by Pearson Education, Inc.
All rights reserved.
No part of this publication may be reproduced, stored in a retrieval system, or transmitted in any form or by any means, electronic, mechanical, photocopying, recording, or otherwise, without the prior permission of the publisher.

Pearson Education, 10 Bank Street, White Plains, NY 10606

Vice president, instructional design: Allen Ascher
Senior acquisitions editor: Marian Wassner
Development editors: Trish Lattanzio, Julie Rouse
Vice president, director of design and production: Rhea Banker
Executive managing editor: Linda Moser
Production editor: Michael Mone
Production supervisor: Liza Pleva
Director of manufacturing: Patrice Fraccio
Senior manufacturing buyer: Dave Dickey
Cover design: Ann France
Text design: Ann France
Text composition: Word & Image Design Studio Inc.
Illustrations: Craig Attebery, p. 50; Crowleart Group, p. 40; Brian Hughes, pp. 9, 10, 15, 17, 23, 24, 30, 44, 49, 59, 64, 86, 91; Dave McKay, p. 97; Suzanne Magensen, pp. 2, 6, 42, 43, 52, 56, 60, 62; Dusan Petricic, pp. 18, 20, 26, 29, 30, 31, 36; NSV Productions, pp. 16, 38, 58, 59, 70, 93, 94, 95; Meryl Treatner, pp. 43, 44; Word & Image Design, pp. 8, 21, 22, 24, 30, 31, 35, 39, 45, 48, 54, 55, 62, 63, 78, 79, 83-85, 87-90, 92, 94, 96, 98-102
Photography: Gilbert Duclos, pp. 34, 39, 66, 68, 74, 76

ISBN: 0-13-094320-7

Printed in the United States of America
1 2 3 4 5 6 7 8 9 10–BAH–07 06 05 04 03 02

LONGMAN ON THE WEB

Longman.com offers online resources for teachers and students. Access our Companion Websites, our online catalog, and our local offices around the world.

Longman English Success offers online courses to give learners flexible study options. Courses cover General English, Business English, and Exam Preparation.

Visit us at longman.com and englishsuccess.com.

Contents

UNIT 1

Your life and work

➤ Practical conversations

1 **➤VOCABULARY** Complete the sentences. Write the letters of each word on the lines.

1. Laura thinks this rain is ___ ◯ ___ _u_ ___, but I like it.

2. The weather is sunny and warm. It's a ___ ___ ___ _g_ ◯ ___ ___ ___ day!

3. You're from Ithaca? So am I! That's ___ _m_ ◯ ___ ___ ___ ___!

4. I really like your dress. It's ___ ___ _a_ ___ ◯ ___ ___ ___ ___.

5. Traffic was ◯ _o_ ___ ___ ___ ___ ___ ___ this morning. I was late for work.

6. You've been cooking for six hours? That's ___ ___ ___ ___ ◯ ___ ___ _b_ ___ ___!

7. Tomas got another promotion? ___ _o_ ___ ' ◯ ___ kidding!

Look at the circled letters. What's the new word? _____

2 Put the conversation in order. Write the number on the line.

___1___ Terrible weather today!

_____ In Austin, Texas.

_____ My husband and I moved here about a year ago.

_____ You know, I don't think we've met. I'm Tina Roche. I live in 3B.

_____ Nice to meet you too, Amy. How long have you been living here?

_____ Yes, it certainly is. Just awful.

_____ Where did you live before that?

_____ Nice to meet you, Tina. I'm Amy Kwan. I live in 5J.

___9___ You're kidding! I lived in Austin for two years. What a small world!

3 ▶ VOCABULARY Complete the sentences. Write the letter on the line.

1. I enjoy working with students. That's why I'm a _____ at Clark Street School.

2. I could never be a _____. I don't like being around people who are sick.

3. You're really good at fixing cars. You should apply for a job as a _____.

4. If you want to be a child care worker, you need to really love _____.

5. Rocco's pretty good at _____. Maybe he should get a job as a technician at Computer World.

6. If you dislike _____, you shouldn't work in a restaurant.

a. cooking
b. taking care of children
c. teacher
d. using a computer
e. mechanic
f. nurse

4 Complete the conversation. Use your own words.

A: Hi, Boris. What are you doing?

B: I'm filling out this job application.

A: How long have you been looking for a job?

B: _____.

This application is for a full-time job as

_____.

A: Wow! That's great. Do you like

_____?

B: Yes, I do. And I'm pretty good at

_____. But I need a favor. Would

you mind writing me a letter of recommendation?

A: _____. I'd be glad to.

B: _____.

➤ Practical grammar

5 Complete each sentence. Use the present perfect continuous form of the verb.

1. The weather is terrible. It _____ *has been raining* _____ for six days!

rain

2. I _____ since I was seventeen years old.

drive

3. How long _____ Sheila _____ at Super Foods?

work

4. We _____ in this neighborhood for about a year.

live

5. How long _____ you _____ for a job?

look

6. I _____ the bus since my car broke down last week.

take

7. Marco _____ on the phone since 9:00.

talk

6 Complete each sentence. Use <u>for</u> or <u>since</u>.

1. We've been driving _____ three hours. Let's stop for lunch.

2. I've been studying English _____ I moved here.

3. Jin has been living in the United States _____ last January.

4. Rita has been using e-mail _____ five years.

5. Mr. Wong has been teaching here _____ 1985.

6. They've been looking for a new apartment _____ almost a month.

7. We've been waiting to see this movie _____ two weeks.

8. I've been buying gas at Superco _____ the Exoco station closed last month.

7 Write a question for each sentence. Use the present perfect continuous.

1. Ellen has been taking Russian classes for six months.

   <u>*How long has Ellen been taking Russian classes?*</u>

2. Alan has been driving a pickup truck for about a year.

   _____

3. We have been shopping at the international supermarket since we moved here.

   _____

4. The technicians have been repairing computers for three years.

   _____

5. Tatiana has been making her own clothes since 1998.

   _____

6. My back has been hurting since last week.

   _____

8 Complete each sentence with a gerund. Use the words from the box.

study	make	work	~~take~~	live	do

1. I like _____*taking*_____ the train. It's fast, and I don't have to worry about traffic.

2. Marie doesn't like _____ in an apartment. She'd like to buy a house.

3. Do you dislike _____ housework? Then call Happy Housekeepers today!

4. My children don't mind _____ because they enjoy school.

5. I'm good at _____ small talk with someone I've just met.

6. Han is great at _____ with people. That's why he's a Customer Service manager.

9 Complete each sentence about <u>yourself</u>. Use gerunds.

1. I love _____ but I'm not very good at it.

2. I can't stand _____.

3. I'm pretty good at _____.

➤ Authentic practice

10 Read. Choose <u>your</u> response. Fill in the ovals.

1. "I really like that jacket. It's the perfect color for you."

   ⓐ Thank you.   ⓑ That's incredible!

2. "Awful weather we're having, isn't it?"

   ⓐ Yes, it is. Gorgeous.   ⓑ Yes, it is. Terrible.

3. "You studied German in Hamburg? That's amazing! So did I!"

   ⓐ Not at all.   ⓑ It's a small world.

4. "I don't believe we've met. I'm Ernesto Diaz."

   ⓐ Hi, Ernesto. I'm Sandra Chen.   ⓑ OK. Not yet.

5. "How did you hear about this position?"

   ⓐ I saw the ad in the newspaper.   ⓑ I really enjoy cooking.

6. "Can you tell me a little more about your skills?"

   ⓐ Well, I don't like cooking or   ⓑ Well, I'm good at working with people.
   cleaning.

11 Complete the sentences. Write the letter on the line.

1. Would you mind _____?

2. I can tell you a little about _____.

3. My sister just _____.

4. If you want to call Joe first, I _____.

5. He's applying for a position _____.

6. Have you been _____?

7. My English has been getting better _____.

a. can't stand working in such a cold place

b. since I started taking classes

c. as a shift supervisor

d. myself

e. don't mind waiting

f. being a reference for me

g. driving a bus long

12 Read the interviewer's questions. Then answer in your <u>own</u> words.

Jose: Good morning. I'm Jose Arroyo. Please call me Jose. What would you like me to call you?

YOU _____

Jose: How did you hear about the position?

YOU _____

Jose: Great. Now would you mind telling me a little about yourself?

YOU _____

Jose: Well, we have several openings right now. When can you give me a list of references?

YOU _____

13 Ask three people who know you well to be a reference for you. Write their information in the chart below. Remember to check with your references for permission to use their names.

	Name	Title	Phone
1.	Address		
2.	Name	Title	Phone
	Address		
3.	Name	Title	Phone
	Address		

14 Which things are OK to do when interviewing for a job? Which ones aren't OK? Check ☑ the correct box.

	OK	Not OK
1. Eating or drinking	❏	❏
2. Bringing a friend with you	❏	❏
3. Arriving a little early	❏	❏
4. Arriving a little late	❏	❏
5. Giving the interviewer your references	❏	❏
6. Talking about your personal problems	❏	❏
7. Wearing simple, neat clothes	❏	❏
8. Wearing a lot of makeup and perfume	❏	❏
9. Asking the interviewer about the salary first	❏	❏
10. Talking about your experience	❏	❏

15 Complete the conversation. Use ideas from Exercise 14 and your <u>own</u> ideas.

A: Guess what? I've got a job interview _____!

B: _____! Congratulations! What kind of job is it?

A: It's for a job as _____.

B: Good for you!

A: I wanted to ask you a favor. This is my first interview, and I'm a little nervous. Do you have any advice for me?

B: Well, _____ is important. And I suggest

_____ and _____.

A: Is there anything I shouldn't do?

B: Definitely. Avoid _____

or _____ And _____ is

a bad idea too.

A: OK. That's good advice. Thanks!

B: Sure. Good luck!

16 Read Ms. Tran's job application. Then check ☑ <u>True</u> or <u>False</u>.

F&L Industries

Employment Application

Date: _____6/30/03_____

Name: _____Tran_____Thuy_____Thi_____
          last   first   middle

Address: _716 Lakeview Dr., #T12____El Segundo, CA____90245_

How long have you been living at this address? ____1____ year(s)

Are you currently employed? Ⓨ / N   If yes, position: _assembler_____

Employer and address: _Miller Electronics, 1701 Eustis St., El Segundo, CA 90246_

How long have you been working for this employer? ___3 yrs.___

If not currently employed, last position held: _____

Dates: from _____ to _____

What type of position are you seeking? _technician_____

What shifts can you work? _X_ 8 a.m.–4 p.m.   _X_ 4 p.m.–12 a.m.   ____ 12 a.m.–8 a.m.

Please list your skills: _I'm good at organizing, working with my hands, and I speak_
___English and Vietnamese._____

	True	False
1. Ms. Tran has a middle name.	☐	☐
2. She has been living at 716 Lakeview Dr. since 1999.	☐	☐
3. Ms. Tran is unemployed right now.	☐	☐
4. She can work any shift.	☐	☐
5. Ms. Tran says she is good at working with her hands.	☐	☐

17 Fill out this job application for <u>yourself</u>.

F&L Industries

Employment Application

Date: _____

Name: _____
          last   first   middle

Address: _____

How long have you been living at this address? _____ year(s)

Are you currently employed? Y / N   If yes, position: _____

Employer and address: _____

How long have you been working for this employer? _____

If not currently employed, last position held: _____

Dates: from _____ to _____

What type of position are you seeking? _____

What shifts can you work? ____ 8 a.m.–4 p.m.   ____ 4 p.m.–12 a.m.   ____ 12 a.m.–8 a.m.

Please list your skills: _____

U N I T   2

Your environment

➤ Practical conversations

1 **➤ VOCABULARY** **Look at the pictures. Then match each picture with a direction. Write the letter on the line.**

 a.    b.    c.    d.

_____   1. Go down the stairs.

_____   2. Take the escalator.

_____   3. It's on the top floor.

_____   4. Take the elevator.    e.   f.

_____   5. Make a left.

_____   6. It's on the ground floor.

_____   7. Go to the end of the hall.    g.   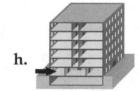 h.

_____   8. Take the second right.

2 **Complete the conversation. Use words from the box.**

in	right	second	~~cafeteria~~	hall	end	elevator

A: Excuse me. Can you tell me how to get to the _____*cafeteria*_____ ?
                                                                    1.

B: Sure. Go to the _____ of the hall. Take the _____
                              2.   3.

   to the third floor. Go down the _____ and make your
                                                4.

   _____ left. The cafeteria will be on your _____ ,
              5.   6.

   _____ Room 210.
              7.

A: Great. Thanks.

3 ➤ *VOCABULARY* **Complete each sentence with <u>on</u>, <u>across from</u>, <u>between</u>, <u>next to</u>, or <u>at the corner of</u>.**

1. Pine Street is _____ Maple and Poplar.

2. The library is _____ Hunter and Redwood.

3. Why don't we meet at the Cineplex? It's _____ the bus terminal.

4. The Farmers' Market is on Maple, _____ Mario's Pizza.

5. The hospital is _____ Fulton and Redwood.

6. There's a great Chinese restaurant _____ Fulton Street. It's _____ the parking garage.

Arbor City Bus Lines

4 **Complete the conversations. Use your <u>own</u> words.**

1. **A:** Excuse me. Can you tell me where _____ is?

   B: Sure. It's _____.

   A: Do you know how to get there by _____?

   B: Yes. Take _____ to _____ and then _____.

   A: Thanks very much.

2. **A:** Would you like to _____ with me _____?

   B: _____. What time do you want to meet?

   A: _____.

   B: OK. And where should I meet you?

   A: _____.

   B: Sounds good. I'll see you then.

➤ Practical grammar

5 **Complete the sentences with directions, warnings, requests, or suggestions.**

1. _Why don't_ you _____ask_____ your boss about that promotion?

2. _____ on the wet floor. You might slip.

3. _____ to the movies. We can walk instead.

4. There's an accident on the corner! _____ 911!

5. _____ the number 8 bus to the library.

6. The escalator is out of order. _____ up the stairs.

7. _____ we _____ next week?

8. _____ me where the meeting is tomorrow.

6 **Put the words in order. Write sentences.**

1. mechanic / ask / the / for / Let's / directions / .

   _____

2. eat / go / tonight / Let's / out / to / not / .

   _____

3. stairs / the / Take / basement / to / the / .

   _____

4. after / us / the / coffee / meeting / Please / for / join / .

   _____

5. mall / class / don't / to / Why / the / we / after / walk / ?

   _____

7 Read what each person says. Then respond with a direction, a warning, a suggestion, or a request. Use your <u>own</u> words.

1. "I'd really like to eat at that new Japanese restaurant."

   (YOU) _____

2. "I'm tired. We've been working since 7:30 this morning."

   (YOU) _____

3. "Could you please tell me how to get to the Customer Service office?"

   (YOU) _____

4. "Should I walk or take the bus?"

   (YOU) _____

5. "Where should we have lunch?"

   (YOU) _____

6. "I don't like my English class."

   (YOU) _____

7. "Our new neighbor, Maria, doesn't know anyone in town."

   (YOU) _____

8 Complete each sentence. Use <u>ask</u> or <u>tell</u> and an infinitive.

1. The bus doesn't run on Sundays. _____ Jaime _____ a taxi.

2. I want to go to the movies tonight. _____ Ms. Rogers _____ with us.

3. The elevator is broken. _____ people _____ the stairs.

4. _____ my parents not _____ a big dinner. I'm not very hungry.

5. Jose is applying for a new job. _____ him _____ his teacher for a letter of recommendation.

➤ Authentic practice

9 **Read. Choose your response. Fill in the ovals.**

1. "Where are you coming from?"

   ⓐ From 9 to 5.   ⓑ From Glenville.

2. "I was wondering if you'd like to come over for dinner this Sunday."

   ⓐ There you go.   ⓑ That sounds great.

3. "Would you mind giving me the number of your house again?"

   ⓐ It's 102.   ⓑ Sure. It's right on the corner.

4. "What floor?"

   ⓐ Four, please.   ⓑ Hold the elevator, please.

5. "I don't know how to get to the restaurant from here."

   ⓐ Ask Andres to give you directions.   ⓑ You can't miss it.

10 **Complete the conversation. Choose the best response. Write the letter on the line.**

A: Hello, Gary? This is Ling from work.

B: _____
   1.

A: Yes. But I need directions to your house.

B: _____
   2.

A: From Olcott Avenue. Across from the school.

B: _____
   3.

A: Left onto Belvale. OK. Then what?

B: _____
   4.

A: Three lights . . . first left . . . Cedar Street

B: _____
   5.

A: What's the number of the house?

B: _____
   6.

A: Got it. Thanks, Gary. See you Saturday.

a. Where are you coming from?

b. Go three lights. Make your first left. That's Cedar Street.

c. Number 44. It's the eighth house on the right.

d. OK. Go east on Olcott and make a left onto Belvale.

e. Hi, Ling. Are you coming to my party on Saturday?

f. Right. Stay on Cedar. My house is just past the drugstore.

11 **Read the sentences. Then choose the word or phrase that has the same meaning as the underlined word. Circle the letter.**

1. Let me tell you some of the "unwritten rules" of elevator <u>etiquette</u>.

   a. food   (b.) politeness   c. buttons

2. You should offer to press buttons for <u>passengers</u> on the other side of the car.

   a. people in the elevator   b. drivers   c. people outside the elevator

3. The <u>simplest</u> way to ask is to say, "What floor?" or "Where are you going?"

   a. worst   b. longest   c. easiest

4. Many people don't like alcoholic <u>beverages</u>.

   a. machines   b. foods   c. drinks

5. When your <u>host</u> offers a drink, just ask for fruit juice or soda.

   a. supervisor   b. employee   c. person having the party

6. It is <u>rude</u> to arrive more than fifteen minutes late to a sit-down dinner party.

   a. impolite   b. not easy   c. friendly

12 **What's your advice? Read the etiquette questions. Then tell each person what to do. Use your <u>own</u> words and ideas.**

1. **Mica:** If someone in an elevator asks me "Where are you going?" what should I say?

   YOU _____

2. **Raquel:** If I'm standing near the buttons in an elevator and another person gets on, what should I do?

   YOU _____

3. **Ivan:** I got an invitation to dinner at a classmate's house. It's for 7:00. What time should I get there?

   YOU _____

4. **Ginger:** I don't drink alcohol. If a friend invites me to a party, what should I do when he offers me a drink?

   YOU _____

13 **Read the directions. Then follow the directions on the map below. Answer the question.**

Start at the corner of Truman Street and Prospect Street. Take the number 3 bus going east. Pass the Luna Restaurant on your right. Don't get off the bus at Jefferson Street. Get off at Adams Street. Walk north on Adams. If you come to Union Street, you're going the wrong way. Go straight and make your fourth right. Go to the end of the street.

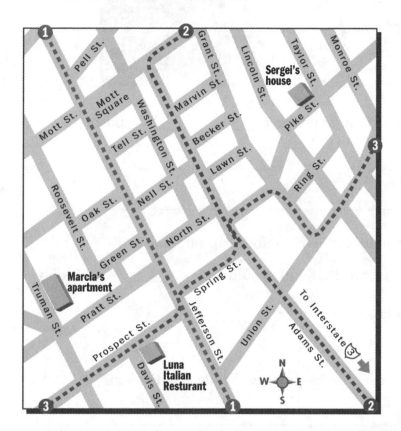

Where are you? At the corner of

_____

and _____.

14 **Marcia wants to buy a used car. Her co-worker, Sergei, has an old car that he wants to sell. He invites Marcia to come and see it on Sunday afternoon. Write directions for Marcia, using the map from Exercise 13. She is going to Sergei's from home. Marcia can walk, drive, or take a bus.**

Dear Marcia,

Here are directions to my house:

_____

_____

_____

_____

_____

_____

See you on _____ at

_____ o'clock.

Sergei

15 Read the invitation. Then complete the paragraphs.

A dinner party!
Time: _6:30_
Date: _May 11_
Place: _35 Grove Street_
RSVP: _929-3430_
Hope you can come!
Marian

_____ would like to invite you to a _____ party
       1.   2.

at her house. The party is on _____, at _____.
                                      3.   4.

The host's address is _____.
                                                        5.

    Under the address on the invitation, there are four capital letters.

They are _____. This means that you should _____ Marian
            6.   7.

to tell her if you can come. Her phone number is _____.
                                                8.

16 Write an invitation for a party you would like to give. Use the ideas in the box or your <u>own</u> ideas.

birthday	graduation	anniversary	retirement

Join us to celebrate _____!

Date: _____

Time: _____

Place: _____

Given by: _____

RSVP: _____

U N I T 3

Your equipment and machines

➤ Practical conversations

1 **➤ VOCABULARY** Look at the pictures. Write the words on the line.

_____   _____   _____   _____

_____   _____   _____   _____

2 Complete the conversation. Use words from the box.

warranty	call	trouble	jammed	speak up
printer	fault	purchased	under	

A: Oh, no! I'm going to get in big _____ now.
1.

B: What's the matter?

A: I think I broke the _____. It's _____ again.
2.   3.

B: Maybe you'd better _____ the help line.
4.

A: But they might think it's my _____.
5.

B: Don't worry. It's always good to _____.
6.

A: You're right. Maybe it's still _____ warranty.
7.

B: Well, do you know when it was _____?
8.

A: Yes. About eight months ago.

B: No problem then. It has a one-year _____ on parts and labor.
9.

3 **Match the statements and responses. Write the letter on the line.**

1. I wonder how much cleanser we have. _____

2. We need to go to Chicago next week. _____

3. I think my computer is frozen. _____

4. That sink is clogged. _____

5. We're out of paper and pencils. _____

a. Why don't I make reservations for us?

b. Maybe we should call maintenance.

c. Let's check stock on the computer.

d. Order more supplies at paperclips.com.

e. Why don't you try restarting it?

4 **Complete the conversations. Use the pictures or your <u>own</u> words.**

1. **A:** I can't believe it!

   B: What's the matter?

   A: The _____ is _____.

   B: Again? That's the third time this week!

   A: I know. And it was just _____ last month.

   B: Well, we'd better _____.

2. **A:** Can you help me?

   B: Sure. _____?

   A: Well, my computer _____ and I have to

   _____.

   B: Did you try _____?

   A: No, I didn't. I'll do that right now.

➤ Practical grammar

5 Complete each sentence in the passive voice. Use the past participle.

1. The Luxell coffee maker was ___*chosen*___ as the Coffee Maker of the Year.
   <u>choose</u>

2. This power saw was _____ at Murphy's Hardware Store.
   <u>buy</u>

3. Was the window _____ when you moved in?
   <u>break</u>

4. This sink was _____ by the night staff.
   <u>fix</u>

5. Were the packages _____ on Tuesday?
   <u>send</u>

6. When were the meeting rooms _____?
   <u>clean</u>

7. We didn't have to pay when the machine was _____ because it was
   <u>service</u>
   still under warranty.

8. The repair or replace order was _____ a week ago, but the copier
   <u>write</u>
   was just _____ this morning.
   <u>repair</u>

6 Complete each sentence in the passive voice.

1. **A:** When was the smoke detector checked?
   B: It _____ in June.

2. **A:** Are the bathrooms cleaned every day?
   B: No, they _____ once a week.

3. **A:** Where was your car taken?
   B: It _____ to Vinny's Auto Repair.

4. **A:** Why was this machine serviced?
   B: It _____ because it jammed again.

5. **A:** Were the computers repaired?
   B: Yes, they _____ last night.

6. **A:** Were these drills made in Mexico?
   B: No, they _____ in China.

7. **A:** Was this floor polisher purchased today?
   B: Yes, it _____ this morning.

7 Look at the answers. Then write questions in the passive voice.

1. A: (your house) _____When was your house painted?_____

   B: It was painted last summer.

2. A: (this computer) _____

   B: It was serviced because it crashed.

3. A: (the sander) _____

   B: It was repaired at Benny's Appliance Shop.

4. A: (these sewing machines) _____

   B: They were cleaned in October.

5. A: (those pictures) _____

   B: They were taken last June.

6. A: (your camera) _____

   B: It was made in Germany.

7. A: (the letter) _____

   B: It was sent by express mail.

8 ➤ *CHALLENGE* **What should be done when these things aren't working? Write repaired or replaced. Use your own opinion.**

Repair
or
replace?

1. A $9 camera should be _____replaced_____.

2. A $300 digital camera should be _____.

3. Dirty oil in your car should be _____.

4. Old tires should be _____.

5. A six-month-old vacuum cleaner should be _____.

6. A coat from 1980 should be _____.

7. A one-year-old computer should be _____.

8. A seven-year-old computer should be _____.

➤ Authentic practice

9 Read. Choose your response. Fill in the ovals.

1. "Fixing this copier is a total waste of time."

   ⓐ Let's start now.   ⓑ You can say *that* again!

2. "This is the third time this washing machine's been serviced this month!"

   ⓐ That's ridiculous.   ⓑ Not a good idea.

3. "Do you know if this stove can be repaired?"

   ⓐ I'll ask maintenance to look at it.   ⓑ I'll check stock.

4. "My computer keeps crashing."

   ⓐ Maybe you should call the help line.   ⓑ They'll think it's my fault.

5. "Maybe I should just say I found it like this when I got here."

   ⓐ It was just fixed!   ⓑ You really should speak up.

10 Read the conversation. Then fill in the service record card.

A: Was the fryer fixed?
B: Yes. The technician was here about an hour ago.
A: That was fast. What was wrong?
B: The temperature control was stuck. It's fine now.
A: Great. Did you fill in the service record?
B: No, I didn't. What should I write?
A: Just write today's date and what was repaired.
B: So I write "temperature control fixed"?
A: Yes, that should do it. And in the warranty column,
    make sure you mark that it was repaired under warranty.
B: OK. I'll take care of it right away.

Benny's Restaurants   Service Record

Item: *Kensico Deep Fryer 5000*

Date	Repair	Under Warranty?
March 4, 2003	*Basket replaced*	Ⓨ N
		Y N

11 Read about the equipment policy for Hot Potato Restaurant Supply. Then check ☑ <u>True</u> or <u>False</u>.

HOT POTATO
Restaurant Supply

Equipment use and safety

- Please take your time when cleaning all equipment. Be careful not to disconnect any wires.
- Notify your manager immediately if there is a problem with any piece of equipment. For your own safety, do not try to fix the equipment yourself. Put an "out of order" sign on the machine, write up a repair or replace order, and report the problem to your manager promptly.
- Never use a piece of equipment you are unfamiliar with. If you aren't sure how to use a machine, ask your manager for assistance.

Failure to report equipment problems or ask for help when needed could result in injury to you and/or your co-workers.

Don't be afraid to report a problem. Your concern about the equipment and your co-workers will be rewarded!
Let's work together to get the job done!

(16)

	True	False
1. The faster you clean, the better.	☐	☐
2. Managers at Hot Potato want to know about problems.	☐	☐
3. You should try to fix a problem yourself before you tell a manager.	☐	☐
4. You should put a sign on any broken machines.	☐	☐
5. It's OK to use equipment you haven't used before.	☐	☐
6. If you don't report an equipment problem, someone could get hurt.	☐	☐
7. If you tell your manager about a problem, you'll always be blamed.	☐	☐

12 Write a response to each statement. Use your <u>own</u> words.

Lisa: Oh, no! I can't believe what I just did!

YOU _____

Lisa: I was trying to fix this machine, and I broke the handle. This is the second time I've done that this month. What should I do?

YOU _____

Lisa: I don't know. Maybe I should just forget about it. I don't want anyone to know I broke it.

YOU _____

13 **Read the warranty. Then complete the paragraphs.**

MicroTastic®

Commercial Microwave Oven

Warranty

All warranty service is to be provided by
an authorized MicroTastic® technician.
For service, call 1-800-MTASTIC.

Length of warranty—MicroTastic® will replace or repair:

Full one-year: from date of purchase	Limited three-year: second through fourth year from date of purchase
Any part that fails because of a defect in materials or workmanship. During this one-year period, all parts and labor will be provided free of charge.	The magnetron tube, if it fails because of a defect in materials or workmanship. During this period, purchaser will be responsible for costs of labor.

The warranty for the MicroTastic Commercial Microwave Oven begins

from the date of _____. If any part fails during the first
                         1.

year you own the microwave, MicroTastic will _____
                                                      2.

or repair the product _____ of charge. This means
                              3.

that the _____ is not responsible for the cost of
               4.

_____ or labor.
        5.

In the second through fourth year of the warranty, only the

_____ is covered. If it fails during this time, this part
        6.

will be replaced or repaired by _____ but the purchaser
                                        7.

will be responsible for the cost of _____.
                                          8.

14 ▸ *CHALLENGE* **Look at the proof-of-purchase card that Mr. Vasilli filled out. Match the questions in the box with his answers. Write each question on the correct line.**

How many other food processors have you owned?
Where was this food processor purchased?
Where will this food processor be used?
~~What is the model number?~~
What was the price paid for this food processor?
When did you purchase this item?
Was this product received as a gift?
What made you decide to purchase a Kitchenelle Food Processor?

PROOF OF PURCHASE

Kitchenelle Food Processor

Please fill in and return the card below to register your Kitchenelle Food Processor. Must be sent in within one month of purchase to activate warranty.

Name   *Germano Vasilli*

Address   *634 Archer Road   Wharton, MA   02144*

1. <u>*What is the model number?*</u>   [*CC93088*]

2. _____   ___ *8* / *20* / *03* ___

3. _____
   ☐ department store   ☐ home center   ☑ discount department store

4. _____
   ☐ yes   ☑ no

5. _____
   ☑ home   ☐ restaurant   ☐ other food business

6. _____
   ☐ none   ☑ 1   ☐ 2 or more

7. _____ $ [*59.95*]

8. _____
   ☐ price   ☑ reputation   ☐ advertising   ☐ family/friend recommendation

UNIT 4

Your customers

➤ Practical conversations

1 ➤ **VOCABULARY** Circle the word that doesn't match.

1. a replacement   a credit   (a customer)   a refund

2. no good   convenient   defective   not up to code

3. a cookie   a crib   a car seat   a stroller

4. faucets   shower heads   zippers   toilets

5. over here   upstairs   below standard   in aisle 3

6. pesticides   complaints   weed killers   motor oil

2 Complete the conversation. Use words from the box.

defective	in the back	anymore	complained
great	have a look	carry	shame

A: Excuse me. Do you _____ Calorific appliances?

1.

B: No, not _____.

2.

A: Really? Why not?

B: A lot of customers _____ about them. Some of them were

3.

_____.

4.

A: That's a _____. My old Calorific stove was really _____.

5.   6.

B: Well, we have a few other models _____ that are just as good.

7.

Would you like to _____?

8.

A: Sure.

3 Complete the sentences. Use your <u>own</u> words and places.

1. You should buy a _____ before your baby is born.

2. _____ is an effective cleaner.

3. _____ cars are no good.

4. The food at _____ is not too good.

5. The food at _____ is fantastic.

6. The most convenient place for me to shop is _____.

4 Complete the conversations. Use your <u>own</u> words.

1. **A:** Can I help you?

   B: Yes, please. I bought this

   _____

   yesterday and it's not working. I think

   it's _____.

   A: I'm sorry. Would you like to get a

   _____?

   B: No, thanks. I'd rather have a

   _____.

   Is that OK?

   A: _____. I'll just need to see your receipt.

2. **A:** Have the Quality brand _____ been discontinued?

   B: Yes, they have.

   A: Why?

   B: _____.

   A: That's _____. They were _____.

   B: That's what everyone said. Can I show you something else?

   A: _____.

➤ Practical grammar

5 Read about Francisco Alvarez. Then write about what he used to do and what he does now.

in the past	now
1. worked part-time	works full-time
2. took the bus to work	drives his own car to work
3. lived with three friends	lives with his wife and baby
4. spent all his money	saves his money in the bank
5. spoke only Spanish	speaks Spanish and English

1. _He used to work part-time. Now he works full-time._
2. _____
3. _____
4. _____
5. _____

6 Write sentences about things you used to do that you don't do now. Use ideas from the box or your own ideas.

stay up late	wake up early	exercise
take a bus	smoke	live in a large city
work in an office	drive a car	go to school in the morning

1. _I used to go to school in the morning. Now I go to school at night._
2. _____
3. _____
4. _____
5. _____

Circle the choice closer in meaning to each sentence.

1. Rapid Flush toilets are as expensive as Lo-Flow toilets.

   a. Lo-Flow toilets are less expensive.   b. Both toilets cost the same.

2. The subway is as fast as the train.

   a. The train is faster than the subway.   b. The train and the subway are both fast.

3. These hammers are not as strong as they used to be.

   a. The hammers were stronger in the past.   b. The hammers are stronger now.

Rewrite the sentences. Use comparisons with _as_.

1. My street is quieter than your street.

   Your street isn't _as quiet as my street_____.

2. High-Tech tools are more expensive than Acme tools.

   Acme tools aren't _____.

3. Infant World cribs are safer than Snug Sleep cribs.

   Snug Sleep cribs aren't _____.

4. The city is more exciting than the suburbs.

   The suburbs aren't _____.

5. Bug-Dead is more effective than Bug-B-Gone.

   Bug-B-Gone isn't _____.

9 Write comparisons using comparative forms. Use your _own_ opinions.

1. Georgia Street / Circle Road

   _Georgia Street is more dangerous than Circle Road._____

2. zippers / buttons

   _____

3. fixing a car / using a computer

   _____

4. apartment / house

   _____

➤ Authentic practice

10 Read. Choose **your** response. Fill in the ovals.

1. "Have you been getting complaints about the new locks?"

   ⓐ Yes. The customers say they're defective.　　ⓑ Yes. The customers say they're fantastic.

2. "What a shame that pet carrier was discontinued. It was really great."

   ⓐ That's what everyone said.　　ⓑ Would you like to have a look?

3. "Could I have a look at the other brands you carry?"

   ⓐ Sure. They're in the back.　　ⓑ We used to, but we don't anymore.

4. "Your tires look a little low."

   ⓐ Can I get a credit instead?　　ⓑ Do you have an air pump?

5. "Is this model being recalled?"

   ⓐ Yes. It's just as good as the old one.　　ⓑ Yes. It has a part that's no good.

11 Who says this? Check ☑ **customer** or **attendant**.

	customer	attendant
1. "Yes, sir?"	❑	❑
2. "Excuse me. Where is your air pump?"	❑	❑
3. "Check the oil?"	❑	❑
4. "You're down a quart."	❑	❑
5. "Fill it up with regular, please."	❑	❑
6. "By the way, your tires look a little low."	❑	❑
7. "That'll bring it to $12.65."	❑	❑
8. "Give me a quart of 15W40."	❑	❑
9. "Do you still carry Smooth Ride motor oil?"	❑	❑

12 Read the newspaper article. Complete the sentences.

The Consumer Product Safety Commission announced today that automotive giant Worldwide Motors is recalling more than 70,000 Hurricane passenger cars. The recall is due to a potentially dangerous defect in the front bumper. Only cars with a 2000 model year are being recalled. Owners of a 2000 Hurricane may take it to any Worldwide dealer, where repairs will be made free of charge.

1. Worldwide Motors is _____ Hurricane passenger cars.
   recalling / replacing

2. More than _____ cars might have a problem.
   2,000 / 70,000

3. Some of the cars have a _____ front bumper.
   defective / convenient

4. Hurricane owners should return their cars to the _____.
   dealer / gas station

5. The company will _____ the car free of charge.
   replace / repair

13 Read the recall letter.

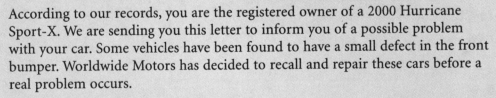

WORLDWIDE MOTORS

Mr. Jonah Ennis
6713 Taylor Rd.
Lee Valley, OR 90610

Dear Mr. Ennis:

According to our records, you are the registered owner of a 2000 Hurricane Sport-X. We are sending you this letter to inform you of a possible problem with your car. Some vehicles have been found to have a small defect in the front bumper. Worldwide Motors has decided to recall and repair these cars before a real problem occurs.

Please bring your vehicle to any Worldwide Motors dealer, and we will repair your car free of charge.

Thank you for choosing a Worldwide vehicle. We appreciate your business.

Sincerely,
Henrietta Fort

Henrietta Fort

Henrietta Fort
Chair and CEO

Now answer the questions. Use the recall letter in Exercise 13.

1. What kind of car does Jonah Ennis have?

   _____

2. Why was the letter sent to Mr. Ennis?

   _____

3. According to the letter, what does Mr. Ennis need to do?

   _____

14 Read the notice about a Household Chemical Clean-up Day program. Then answer the questions. Check ☑ <u>True</u> or <u>False</u>

Dispose of household chemicals properly and protect Woodside's water supply!

On Saturday, May 4, Woodside will hold its annual Household Chemical Clean-up Day at the following locations:

Location	Time
State Park	9 a.m. – 3 p.m.
Woodside Community College	8 a.m. – 2 p.m.
Material Recovery Facility	10 a.m. – 6 p.m.

Items accepted (Note: All chemicals must be in their original labeled containers.)
- Basic household chemicals (glass cleaner, cleansers, furniture polish)
- Pesticides / insecticides
- Weed killer
- Most automotive fluids (antifreeze, brake fluid, gasoline)
- Car tires (maximum of 10)
- Fire extinguishers
- Rechargeable batteries

Items not accepted and what to do with them:
- Paint: Let cans air dry and dispose of with household trash.
- Motor oil: Take to your local gas station or motor oil retail outlet.
- Car batteries: Take to a local scrap metal dealer or auto repair shop.
- Non-rechargeable batteries: Dispose of with household trash.
- Empty chemical containers: Dispose of with household trash.

<u>Remember</u>: Improper disposal of items like pesticides and motor oil could damage our water supply. Never pour these items down the sink or into the sewer. Anyone caught violating EPA rules will be subject to a large fine.

Help protect our environment today for a better tomorrow!

		True	False
1.	The household clean-up day is on May 14.	❑	❑
2.	There are three places where items can be dropped off.	❑	❑
3.	It's OK to pour pesticides down the sink.	❑	❑
4.	Used motor oil should be thrown in the trash.	❑	❑
5.	People who don't follow EPA rules are breaking the law.	❑	❑

15 What's your advice? Tell each person what to do.

1. "These paint cans are empty but still wet inside. What should I do with them?"

   YOU _____

2. "What should I do with these used car batteries?"

   YOU _____

3. "How do we dispose of these empty glass cleaner bottles?"

   YOU _____

16 ▸ _CHALLENGE_ **Write a complaint letter about something you bought.**

You recently bought a product at Buy-Lo Department Store and you are unhappy with it. You decide to write a complaint letter to the company.

Remember to include the following information in your letter:
- what you purchased
- when and where you bought it
- what the problem is
- how you would like the company to make good (offer a refund, an exchange, a credit, or a repair)

Dear Sir or Madam:

I'm writing to complain about _____

_____

_____

_____

_____

I'm very disappointed with _____

_____

_____

_____

                                    Sincerely, _____

UNIT 5

Your time

➤ Practical conversations

1 **➤VOCABULARY** Complete the sentences. Write the missing letters on the lines.

1. The waiters at Good Grub Restaurant are paid $3.00 an hour, plus _t_ __ __ _s_ .

2. When I have to work overtime, I get paid _t_ __ __ _e_ and a _h_ __ __ _f_ .

3. Companions are often paid a salary, plus _r_ __ __ _m_ and _b_ __ __ __ __ _d_ .

4. Taxi drivers are usually paid by the _t_ __ __ _p_ , plus tips.

5. _M_ __ __ __ __ __ _m_ _w_ __ __ _e_ is $5.15 per hour.

6. Because we worked on a holiday, the company paid us _d_ __ __ __ __ _e_ _t_ __ __ _e_ .

2 What occupations are paid this way? Complete the chart. Use occupations from your book and your **own** ideas.

Paid by the hour, plus tips	Paid by the job or trip	Paid by the week
a waiter		

3 Put the conversation in order. Write the number on the line.

__1__ Hey, Julio! Guess what? I got a job!

_____ Plus tips?

_____ And how will you be paid?

_____ They're a great company. Is it full-time or part-time?

_____ You did? That's terrific! What kind of job is it?

_____ Full-time. Nine to five.

_____ By the hour.

_____ I'll be a mover for Hercules Moving Company.

__9__ Yes. And I get time and a half if I work on weekends.

4 Look at the underlined words and phrases. Match each underlined word or phrase with its meaning. Write the letter on the line.

1. I have to <u>run an errand</u>. _____   a. sick

2. I need to <u>reschedule</u> our meeting. _____   b. a place to sleep and food

3. Yuri's <u>not feeling well</u> today. _____   c. after work hours

4. Please do that <u>on your own time</u>. _____   d. if it's not

5. I also get <u>room and board</u>. _____   e. go someplace to buy or do things

6. I'd like to <u>make a note of it</u>. _____   f. change to a different time

7. <u>Unless</u> it's an emergency, you should do that later. _____   g. write something down so that you will remember it

5 Complete the conversations. Use your <u>own</u> words.

1. A: _____? Hi, it's _____.

    I'm sorry, but I have to reschedule our _____.

    I _____.

    B: _____. When do you want to reschedule?

    A: Will _____ work?

    B: _____. That's great for me. I'll see you _____.

    A: Thanks, _____.

2. A: Excuse me. Do you know if it's OK to

    _____?

    B: Well, unless it's an emergency, the supervisors expect

    you to do that _____.

    A: And what if I need to _____?

    B: It's also not a good idea to do that on company time.

    Why don't you do that _____?

➤ Practical grammar

6 Complete the paragraph with verbs and infinitives.

Tick Tock
CLOCK COMPANY _____

Overtime Policy   [Policies and Procedures]

If you _**need to work**_ overtime to meet a deadline, _____
     1. need / work   2. remember / ask

your supervisor for permission first. _____ him or her know when you
                                           3. Be sure / let

_____ in the office and how many hours of overtime you _____.
    4. plan / be   5. want / work

Also, _____ your supervisor sign your time sheet.
    6. not forget / have

(23)

7 Look at the answers. Then complete the questions. Use verbs and infinitives.

1. **A:** When do you _plan to call your family_ ?
   B: I plan to call them on Sunday morning.

2. **A:** Why did Jisela _____?
   B: She decided to take the job because it pays a salary, plus room and board.

3. **A:** What did you _____?
   B: I forgot to ask Mr. Kwan about overtime.

4. **A:** Where do you _____?
   B: We need to go to the Human Resources office at break time.

5. **A:** What do they _____?
   B: They want to run some errands tonight.

8 Answer the questions. Use your <u>own</u> ideas.

1. What do you sometimes forget to do?

   _____

2. What do you always remember to do?

   _____

3. Where do you plan to go this weekend?

   _____

9 Complete each sentence with an object and an infinitive.

1. Selina didn't come to school today. I expect ____*her to come*____ to school tomorrow.

2. This is Penny's first day at work. Let's invite _____ lunch with us.

3. Our company doesn't allow _____ personal calls on company time.

4. Mark's not feeling well. He asked _____ today's meeting.

5. Before Jorge's interview, we reminded _____ about overtime.

6. The children didn't finish their work this morning. Please tell

_____ it now.

10 ▶**CHALLENGE** **Pablo is taking a few vacation days to go see his family in Mexico. Read the requests Pablo and his co-workers make. Rewrite each request. Use the verbs in parentheses.**

1. (ask) Ms. Rivas *asks Pablo to send a postcard when he arrives* .

2. (remind) Pablo's boss _____ .

3. (tell) His co-worker, Barry, _____ .

4. (ask) Pablo _____ .

5. (want) His co-worker, Hanna _____ .

➤ Authentic practice

11 **Read. Choose <u>your</u> response. Fill in the ovals.**

1. "The pay is minimum wage to start, with a raise after six months."

   ⓐ Should I do that on my own time?   ⓑ And is there overtime?

2. "Congratulations on your promotion to assistant manager."

   ⓐ Certainly.   ⓑ Thanks.

3. "How are you expected to dress?"

   ⓐ I'd like to wear a dress.   ⓑ We wear a white shirt and black pants.

4. "If Richard calls in sick again, can you fill in for him?"

   ⓐ When do you want to reschedule?   ⓑ No problem.

5. "Do I need to give advance warning if I want to take a personal day?"

   ⓐ Yes, unless it's an emergency.   ⓑ Yes, if it's an emergency.

12 **Which things are OK to do at work? Which ones aren't OK? Check ☑ the correct box.**

	OK	Not OK
1. Arrive early for work	❑	❑
2. Come back late from lunch	❑	❑
3. Ask your boss for permission before taking a personal day	❑	❑
4. Do personal business on company time	❑	❑
5. Give your boss advance warning if you can't be on time	❑	❑
6. Expect your supervisor to tolerate lateness	❑	❑
7. Make a phone call at work because your son is sick	❑	❑

13 Read about the minimum wage taken from the Fair Labor Standards Act website. Then complete the sentences.

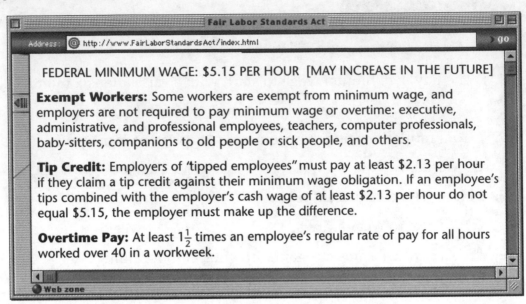

1. According to the website, federal _____ is $5.15 per hour.

2. If someone is an _____ worker, the employer does not

    have to pay that person minimum wage or overtime.

3. A _____ employee must be paid at least $2.13 per hour.

4. If an employee's cash wage plus _____ is not equal to

    $5.15, then the employer must _____ the difference.

5. An employer must pay an employee _____ pay if the

    employee works over 40 hours in a workweek.

14 Read about the people. Then answer <u>yes</u> or <u>no</u>.

1. Eddie is applying for a job as a companion to an older person. Eddie will work at

    the older person's home and her family will pay him $4.00 an hour, plus room and

    board. Do they have to pay Eddie minimum wage? _____

2. Lubna is a hotel housekeeper. If she works 45 hours in a week, does Lubna's

    employer have to pay her overtime? _____

3. Rachel is a hairdresser and gets paid minimum wage, plus tips. One day, she

    doesn't get any tips. Does Rachel's employer have to give her a higher salary for

    that day? _____

15 **Read the want ads.**

HELP WANTED	HELP WANTED	HELP WANTED
Now Hiring Medical Technicians, F/T Medicaid # needed. $30/hr. Time + 1/2 for OT. General Hospital (201) 555-6345 **Baby-sitter Wanted** FT, live-in to care for 2 children. Monday-Friday. $525/wk + room and board. Call (914) 555-0967 after 6pm	***** SALES REPS ***** Earn $12.50-$50 per hour (FT) Must have 3 yrs experience Evenings & weekends a must Call (914) 555-3482 **PARKING ATTENDANT** P/T, $5.15/hr. + tips (20 hrs. per wk.) Shift: 7pm-11pm. 2x on Sundays & holidays. Apply in person at EZ Parking, 125 Vine St.	**PART TIME** Office Asst. for busy office. Approx. 24 hrs/week (days). $18 per hr. Flexible schedule. No exp. necessary. Good phone skills a must. (222) 555-1459 **Now Hiring** Looking for someone with minimum 3 yrs experience

Circle these abbreviations in the ads. What do they mean? Write the words on the line.

1. P/T   = *part-time*   6. OT   = _____

2. #   = _____   7. 2x   = _____

3. hr   = _____   8. yrs   = _____

4. FT   = _____   9. time + 1/2 = _____

5. +   = _____   10. wk   = _____

16 ▶ *CHALLENGE* **Read about each person. Choose the best job for each one. Use the want ads from Exercise 15.**

1. Alene Alon needs a full-time job and a place to live. She can't work on the weekends because she has school.

   _____

2. Dmitri Pavovich needs to earn at least $425 per week. He lives with his elderly mother and only has a companion for her three days a week. _____

3. Arturo Ruiz is looking for a part-time job. He already has a day job. He'd like a job where he can work some overtime.

   _____

17 How much do they get paid? Complete the chart.

Position	regular pay	time and a half	double time
medical billing assistant	$5.20		
busboy (before tips)			$8.20
school custodian		$11.25	

18 Talk to Heather in Human Resources about a job you saw in the newspaper.
Complete the conversation. Use your <u>own</u> words.

Heather: Which job are you interested in?

YOU _____

Heather: OK. What would you like to know about the job?

YOU _____

Heather: It's full-time. Monday through Friday. The job starts at 7 a.m. and ends at 3 p.m. You might have to work later on some days. If you do, you'll get overtime pay.

YOU _____

Heather: We pay minimum wage to start, with raises for good performance. When would you like to come in for an interview?

YOU _____

Heather: That's good for me. I'll see you then.

YOU _____

UNIT 6

Your supplies and resources

➤ Practical conversations

1 **➤ VOCABULARY** Complete the sentences. Write the letters of each word in the boxes. Then look at the gray boxes ▨. What's the new word?

1. Soda is on sale, but you need this _____.

2. We carry spaghetti sauce in _____ but not in cans.

3. I usually buy milk in a half-gallon _____.

4. That price is too low. Maybe it's a _____.

5. We need a lot of onions. Let's get the big _____.

6. Three for a dollar! That's a _____!

7. You can get juice in a can or a _____.

Write the new word: _____

2 **➤ CHALLENGE** Complete the chart. List foods and drinks that are sold in the different types of packages. Use foods and drinks from the book and your <u>own</u> ideas.

Can	Jar	Bag	Bottle	Box	Container
tuna					milk

3 Complete the conversation. Use the words from the box.

mistake	boxes	coupon	bargain	each
crackers	loaf	two	ounce	sale price

A: I'm going to the supermarket. Do you need anything?

B: Yes, thanks. I need a _____ of bread
1.

and some _____, too.
2.

A: How many _____ do you want?
3.

B: Well, the flyer says that Krispies are _____ for 99 cents.
4.

A: That must be a _____. They're usually $1.59 _____.
5.   6.

B: No. Look at the flyer. It's a 16-_____ box.
7.

A: Wow! What a _____! I think I'll get some, too.
8.

B: Don't forget to take the _____! You won't get the
9.

_____ without it!
10.

4 Complete the conversation. Use your <u>own</u> words.

A: I really need to buy _____ but I don't have time to

_____.

B: Can I make a suggestion? Why don't you _____?

A: How do I do that?

B: Call _____. Or you can log on to _____.

A: That's a great idea. Thanks!

5 Answer the questions about <u>yourself</u>.

1. How do you buy clothes? _____

2. Do you sometimes shop by phone or online? Why or why not? _____

   _____

3. What things can you buy online? _____

4. What's the best bargain you've found at the store? How much does it usually cost?

   _____

➤ Practical grammar

6 **Complete each conclusion. Use <u>must</u> and the verb.**

1. Lena had to reschedule our lunch. She _____*must be*_____ very busy.
   be

2. David always buys the meatless spaghetti sauce. He _____ meat.
   not eat

3. Carla wants to be a teacher. She _____ working with children.
   like

4. My aunt only buys sale items. She _____ a bargain.
   love

5. The new Foodway Store is very large. They _____ a really
   have
   good selection.

7 **Write a conclusion with <u>must</u> and a verb. Use your <u>own</u> words.**

1. She bought 20 cans of soup today.

   She *must like soup* _____.

2. Andrew takes the bus every day.

   He _____.

3. Giorgio asked me to fill in for him tonight.

   He _____.

4. The busboys only earn $2.50 an hour.

   They _____.

5. My mother always shops at Bargain Town.

   She _____.

8 **Look at the pictures. Then write a conclusion.**

1.   2.   3.

1. *They must need a new car.* _____

2. _____

3. _____

9 Complete each exclamation with __What__.

1. _____ warranty! Let's look for another machine.
   terrible

2. _____ shower heads! At that price, they must work well.
   expensive

3. _____ dinner! Your father's a terrific cook!
   delicious

4. _____ house! It must be very expensive.
   gigantic

5. _____ letter of recommendation. Your boss must like you a lot.
   nice

10 For each situation, write an exclamation with __What__.

1. Your brother just bought you two tickets to see a movie tonight.

   (YOU) _What fun!_____

2. Your friend is wearing a new dress. It's very beautiful.

   (YOU) _____

3. You just bought four bottles of juice for $3.00.
   They usually cost $1.50 each.

   (YOU) _____

4. You eat at a new restaurant. The food is very good.

   (YOU) _____

5. It's cold and raining outside. It's been raining for three days.

   (YOU) _____

6. A new store opens near your house. It has a large selection.

   (YOU) _____

➤ Authentic practice

11 Read. Choose <u>your</u> response. Fill in the ovals.

1. "What a huge job! We'll never finish it."

   ⓐ Can I make a suggestion?   ⓑ That must be a mistake.

2. "It's easy to figure out the best buy if you check the unit price."

   ⓐ What's in it?   ⓑ Why didn't *I* think of that?

3. "The larger the package, the cheaper the unit price."

   ⓐ Wow, that *is* a problem.   ⓑ Really?

4. "I don't feel like going to the store, but I really need a new coffee maker."

   ⓐ Order it by phone or online.   ⓑ Actually, that won't work.

5. "I'm thinking about ordering our uniforms online."

   ⓐ You can say *that* again!.   ⓑ What a great idea!

12 ➤**CHALLENGE** Look at the coupons. Complete the sentences. Write the letter on the line.

1. To use the pizza coupon, you have to buy _____.   a. 5/12/04

2. You can only get two pizzas _____.   b. one 24-oz. can

3. For the Family Chicken Dinner special, you need _____.   c. brand

4. The special on the chicken dinner is good until _____.   d. a coupon

5. With the soup coupon, you get $1.00 off when you buy _____.   e. two pizzas

6. The soup coupon is only good for the Wholesome _____.   f. per person

13 Label each item on the unit pricing label. Write the letter on the line.

1. product name _____
2. package price _____
3. UPC code _____
4. unit price _____
5. unit of measure _____

14 Complete the sentences about unit pricing and units of measure. Circle the letter.

1. The price of a unit in a package is the _____.

   a. unit price   b. package price

2. Unit pricing helps you _____.

   a. compare prices   b. choose the best product

3. Unit pricing CANNOT _____.

   a. help you save money   b. tell you which item tastes better

4. You find unit prices _____.

   a. on the nutritional label   b. on the shelf tag

5. Trash bags are sold by _____.

   a. count   b. volume

6. An example of a product sold by weight is _____.

   a. meats   b. paper towels

15 Complete the chart. Figure out the unit prices.

product	package price	package size	unit price
1. potatoes	$3.00	5 lbs.	60 cents per pound
2. window cleaner	$2.40	24 ozs.	
3. cookies	$3.00	1 pound	
4. writing paper	$6.00	20 pads	
5. ice cream	$4.00	16 ozs.	
6. AA batteries	$4.80	8 batteries	

16 What matters most to you when you're shopping for food? Rate the following by how important they are to you.

	Very important	Somewhat important	Not important
1. nutrition	☐	☐	☐
2. personal tastes	☐	☐	☐
3. quality	☐	☐	☐
4. convenience	☐	☐	☐
5. storage space	☐	☐	☐
6. economy	☐	☐	☐

17 Match the word with the abbreviation. Write the letter on the line.

1. quantity _____   a. EA

2. each _____   b. RL

3. box _____   c. DZ

4. one dozen _____   d. PK

5. pack _____   e. BX

6. roll _____   f. QTY

18 You're an office assistant for State Bank at 1440 Commerce Street in Cleveland, Ohio. Your boss has left you a note about some supplies she needs you to order. Fill out the order form. Use your <u>own</u> name and the abbreviations from Exercise 17.

Hi,

I'm running low on office supplies. Please order the following items:

3 dozen blue ballpoint pens (medium) [Item #425BP]

2 black vinyl binders (2") [Item #671BB]

2 rolls of tape [Item #593ST]

4 packs of index cards (4" x 6") [Item #180IC]

3 boxes of jumbo paper clips [Item #247JC]

Thanks,

Ms. Wang

Top Line Office Products

Submitted by _____

Company name _____

Billing address _____

ITEM NUMBER	QTY	UM	DESCRIPTION

Thank You For Your Order!

UNIT 7

Your relationships

➤ Practical conversations

1 **➤ VOCABULARY** Complete the sentences. Use words from the box.

bring a dog to the park	put the trash cans here	turn down the TV
move your car	park in the managers' lot	turn right on red

1. I can't find any other parking spaces. Is it OK to _____?

2. Is it OK to _____ if I keep him on a leash?

3. I'm trying to sleep. Would it be possible for you to _____?

4. Is it OK if I _____? Or should I bring them to the curb?

5. Do you know if it's legal to _____ here if there are no cars coming?

6. Would it be possible for you to _____? I can't get out of my driveway.

2 What are the rules and laws where you live? Check ☑ **yes**, **no** or **I don't know**.

Is it illegal to. . . ?	yes	no	I don't know
1. let a dog off the leash			
2. make a right turn on red			
3. drive a car when you're fifteen			
4. drink alcohol when you're nineteen			
5. use a cell phone when you're driving			
6. smoke in a restaurant			
7. park on the street overnight			

No overnight parking
1 a.m. to 6 a.m.

$50 fine

3 Match the pictures and the sentences. Write the letter on the line.

1.  2.  3.  4.  5. COURTHOUSE

____   ____   ____   ____   ____

    a. My brother's getting married this weekend.

    b. Elena's not here. She had a death in the family.

    c. My sister-in-law is having a baby in May!

    d. Tina and Ramon are getting a divorce.

    e. Raul lost his job. His company closed down.

4 Complete the conversations. Use your <u>own</u> words.

1. **A:** Hi, _____. How _____?

    B: _____. What's new with you?

    A: Well, _____!

    B: Wow! _____! That *is* big news.

2. **A:** What's wrong? You look really _____.

    B: Actually, _____.

    A: _____. Can I do anything to help you?

    B: _____.

➤ Practical grammar

5 Write your <u>own</u> judgments. Use a word or phrase from each column.

It's	important wrong polite inconvenient illegal hard not easy	to	park in a fire lane offer sympathy when a friend has bad news make small talk at work apologize for your behavior know how to use unit pricing speak up when you've made a mistake be inconsiderate go to the supermarket every day

1. *It's illegal to park in a fire lane.* _____

2. _____

3. _____

4. _____

5. _____

6. _____

6 Rewrite each sentence. Express the ideas in another way.

1. <u>Parking a large car</u> is difficult.

   It's difficult to park a large car. _____

2. I'm sorry, but <u>smoking in the building</u> is illegal.

   _____

3. In spring, <u>getting married</u> outdoors is wonderful.

   _____

4. <u>Meeting new people</u> isn't always easy.

   _____

5. <u>Talking loudly</u> on the phone is impolite.

   _____

6. <u>Buying clothes online</u> is really convenient.

   _____

7 Complete the sentences. Use your <u>own</u> words.

1. In this country, it's impolite to _____.

2. It's difficult to ask someone to _____.

3. It isn't right to _____.

4. I think it's important to always _____.

5. When you are in a hurry, it's hard to _____.

6. I don't think it's bad to _____.

8 Now write questions you can ask a partner.

1. <u>In your country, is it polite to arrive at a friend's house late?</u>

2. _____

3. _____

4. _____

➤ Authentic practice

9 **Read. Choose your response. Fill in the ovals.**

1. "Do you think it would be possible to close the window? It's a little cold in here."

   ⓐ Of course.   ⓑ Is there anything wrong?

2. "Why don't you just ask them to keep it down?"

   ⓐ I'm glad to hear that.   ⓑ I don't want to be rude.

3. "What's bothering Thi? She looks really down lately."

   ⓐ She's getting a promotion.   ⓑ She's getting a divorce.

4. "Could I ask you a big favor?"

   ⓐ Sure. What do you need?   ⓑ Not really, but I appreciate it.

5. "Is the music too loud for you?"

   ⓐ A little. Would it be possible to turn it down?   ⓑ I'm sorry. I didn't realize that.

10 **Complete the conversation. Write the letter on the line.**

A: My co-worker, Sally, is really lazy.

B: _____
   1.

A: She never refills the cleaning cart. When I start my shift, I have to go to the supply room to restock. Then I'm late getting started.

B: _____
   2.

A: You're supposed to restock them at the end of your shift. That's the rule.

B: _____
   3.

A: I don't know. It's just so hard for me to talk to people, because I worry about my English.

B: _____
   4.

A: OK, I'll give it a try. Thanks.

B: _____
   5.

a. Maybe she just doesn't know the rule. Why don't you talk to her?

b. Don't worry. Just be polite and explain what the problem is. I'm sure she'll understand.

c. No problem. Good luck!

d. Lazy? What do you mean?

e. Hmm. What's the policy on refilling the carts?

11 Read the sentences. Then choose the word or phrase that is closest in meaning to the underlined word(s). Circle the letter.

1. If my dog stays inside too long, he <u>barks</u> and bothers the neighbors.

   a. sleeps   **b.** breaks the rules   **(c.)** makes a loud noise

2. There are some things it's important to <u>be aware of</u>, no matter where you live.

   a. have   **b.** know   **c.** practice

3. It's a bad idea to leave young children at home <u>unsupervised</u>.

   a. without an adult   **b.** without rules   **c.** with an adult

4. Although laws <u>differ</u> from place to place, you must have a license for a gun.

   a. are the same   **b.** are important   **c.** are different

5. It's not <u>acceptable</u> to be unaware of community rules and laws.

   a. a problem   **b.** OK   **c.** important

6. <u>Ignorance</u> of the law is not an excuse for breaking the rules.

   a. not knowing   **b.** following   **c.** breaking

12 Match each sign with a sentence. Write the letter on the line.

a. 2 HR METER PARKING 6 am–10 pm Mon-Sat

b. NO TURN ON RED

c. LEFT TURN YIELD ON GREEN

d. $50 FINE

e. NO PARKING LOADING ZONE

f. SPEED 15mph WHEN FLASHING

g. PERMIT PARKING ONLY

1. If no traffic is coming, you can turn left without a green arrow. _____

2. You can't park here if you don't have a permit. _____

3. If you park here on Sunday, you don't have to put money in the meter. _____

4. Trucks load and unload here. We'd better move the car. _____

5. If you don't want to pay a fine, don't litter! _____

6. At this corner, you can't turn right when the light is red. _____

7. When the light is flashing, you have to drive slowly here. _____

13 Read the conversation. Then answer the questions.

TOWN OF SAN LUIS
COURTS AND APPEALS

You are hereby charged with a violation of the laws of the town of San Luis.

DATE OF VIOLATION: *Thursday, July 17th, 2003*
SITE: *corner of Tulip Ave and Route 440*
NATURE OF VIOLATION: *Failure to stop at a red light*
VEHICLE LICENSE NUMBER: *AOM 241*
REGISTERED TO: *Otis Rayburn*
31507 Mills St.
Fort Worth, TX 79703

If you wish to dispute this ticket, you may write to the Division of Courts and Appeals
or appear in person on the court date listed below.

[ACM 241]

Otis: Look at this! I got a traffic ticket in the mail.
Karen: You did? What is it for?
Otis: It says it's for running a red light last Thursday in San Luis. It's one of those red light camera tickets.
Karen: Red light camera ticket? What's that?
Otis: Well, there's a camera at the intersection, and it takes pictures of cars that go through the light after it turns red. They look at the license plate, and a computer sends a ticket to the owner of the car.
Karen: Well, did you do it?
Otis: No! I wasn't even in San Luis last week.
Karen: Did you let anyone else use your car?
Otis: No. In fact, last Thursday I didn't drive to work. I took the bus instead.
Karen: Are you sure that's <u>your</u> car in the picture?
Otis: Let's see . . . no, it's not! The license plate on this car is ACM 241. Mine is AOM 241. This must be a mistake!

1. What did Otis get in the mail?

   a. a ticket   **b.** a letter

2. Why did he get it?

   a. for turning right on red   **b.** for running a red light

3. Where was the ticket from?

   a. San Remon   **b.** San Luis

4. How does Otis know he didn't break the law?

   a. He walked to work that day. **b.** He took the bus that day.

5. What's the license plate number of the car that <u>did</u> break the law?

   a. ACM 241   **b.** AOM 241

14 Look at the picture. Read the signs. Write sentences about the rules and laws.

1. It's illegal to *not wear a helmet when riding a bike.*

2. It's illegal to _____

3. It's illegal to _____

4. It's illegal to _____

5. It's illegal to _____

6. It's illegal to _____

UNIT 8
Your health and safety

➤ Practical conversations

1 **➤VOCABULARY** **Match the sentence(s) in the left column with a sentence in the right column. Write the letter on the line.**

1. The carton says April 1. Today is April 4. __d__

2. This can of beans should be much cheaper. _____

3. This milk is too old. _____

4. The meat's not cooked very much. _____

5. The meat was cooked for a long time. _____

6. It's not spoiled. _____

a. It's not fresh.

b. It's well done.

c. It's OK.

d̶. The sell-by date is expired.

e. It's rare.

f. It's marked wrong.

2 **Complete the sentences. Use words from the box.**

sell-by date	return	spoiled	medium	fish
take it back		fresh	rare	receipt

1. **A:** Look! I just bought this _____, and it's _____.

　　　　　　　　　　　　　　　　　　　　　　1.　　　　　　　　　　　　　　　　2.

   B: No wonder. Look, the _____ was last week.

　　　　　　　　　　　　　　　　3.

   A: You're kidding! I guess I'll _____ it and get another package.

　　　　　　　　　　　　　　　　　　　　　4.

   B: Don't forget to bring the _____.

　　　　　　　　　　　　　　　　　　5.

2. **A:** Is something wrong?

   B: Yes. My steak is too _____. I wanted it _____.

　　　　　　　　　　　　　　　　6.　　　　　　　　　　　　　　　　7.

I don't like it red.

   A: Actually, my salad isn't very _____, either.

　　　　　　　　　　　　　　　　　　　　8.

   B: Let's ask the waiter to _____.

　　　　　　　　　　　　　　　　　9.

   A: Good idea.

3 Complete the sentences. Write the missing letters on the lines.

1. The number of times a day you take a medicine is the _d _ _ _ _ e_ .

2. Instructions for taking your medicine are on the _l _ _ _ l_ .

3. Did the clerk at the pharmacy give you a patient information _s _ _ _ t_ ?

4. Before you take any medicine, read the _i _ _ _ _ _ _ _ _ _ _ _ s_ .

5. Can you take this if you have a high fever? Check the _w _ _ _ _ _ _ _ s_ .

6. My doctor gave me a _p _ _ _ _ _ _ _ _ _ _ _ n_ for my insomnia.

7. Don't use the medicine after the date it _e _ _ _ _ _ _ s_ .

8. The dosage is one _c _ _ _ _ _ _ e_ in the morning and one before bedtime.

4 Look at the labels. Then complete the sentences. Write the letter on the line.

Secutab
Take 1 capsule
just before bedtime,
only as needed,
for insomnia.

Bactoz
Apply to clean affected area
twice a day for rash

Arrocillin
Aku, Dorothy
Take 1 capsule
3 x daily.

Amocid
Truong, Lily
One teaspoon
twice daily
for ear infection

1. Arrocillin is taken _____.

2. Bactoz is medication for _____.

3. The patient needs to take Amocid _____.

4. Secutab and Arrocillin are taken in _____.

a. two times a day

b. capsules

c. three times a day

d. rashes

5 Complete the conversation. Use your <u>own</u> words.

A: I picked up the prescription for your _____.

B: Great, thanks. I really need it.

A: _____.

B: _____?

A: That's right.

B: Are there any other instructions?

A: Yes, they're on _____.

➤ Practical grammar

6 **Write the possessive adjective that corresponds to each subject pronoun.**

1. They think ____*their*____ appointment is on Saturday morning.

2. He lost _____ receipt, so he can't return the chicken.

3. You need to pick up _____ prescription before 5:00 p.m.

4. I called _____ doctor because I had a bad infection.

5. We like _____ vegetables to be very fresh.

6. Ms. Miller sent _____ steak back because it was too rare.

7 **Combine the sentences to make one sentence. Use possessive nouns.**

1. My mother has back pain. It's getting worse.

   My mother's back pain is getting worse.

2. Mrs. Singh is here. Is her prescription ready?

   _____

3. This bag has a sell-by date. It was three weeks ago.

   _____

4. The pharmacists wear uniforms. They're white and blue.

   _____

5. These customers had complaints. Piotr took care of it.

   _____

8 **Match the items with the people. Write sentences using possessive pronouns.**

1. Juan is a cook. *The fryer is his.* _____

2. Angelica is a child care worker. _____

3. Bernie and Eva are plumbers. _____

4. Giovanni is a mover. _____

5. Hamida is a cashier. _____

Complete each sentence.

1. Those must be _____ shopping bags.
   our / ours

2. _____ prescription was very expensive.
   Your / Yours

3. _____ lunch was fine, but Marcela complained about _____.
   My / Mine   her / hers

4. Jai is using Clearox, and _____ rash is much better.
   her / hers

5. My phone's not working. Would it be possible for me to use _____?
   your / yours

6. They're great dogs. But they don't think they're _____.
   my / mine

   They think I'm _____.
   their / theirs

10 ►*CHALLENGE* **Read the clues. Write the names on the lines.**

_____ Lauren _____ _____ _____ _____
    1.   2.   3.   4.   5.   6.

Lauren's son, Tony, is on the left.
Mindy is between her brother-in-law and her brother.
Tony's mother is next to his father, Henry.
Tasha is on the right, next to her husband.
Lauren's brother, Tristen, is between his sister, Mindy, and his wife.

➤ Authentic practice

11 **Read. Choose your response. Fill in the ovals.**

1. "I ordered this hamburger well done."

   ⓐ I'm sorry. Let me take it back.   ⓑ Is everything OK?

2. "Did my doctor call in my prescription yet?"

   ⓐ Yes. It's ready for you now.   ⓑ Yes, they do. What about yours?

3. "I can't believe you're doing that!"

   ⓐ What about yours?   ⓑ What's wrong?

4. "Aren't you supposed to take that on an empty stomach?"

   ⓐ Yes. I'll take it just before lunch.   ⓑ Yes. I'll take it to the pharmacy.

5. "Never slice vegetables and raw chicken on the same cutting board."

   ⓐ Why not?   ⓑ What are the directions?

12 **Read the conversation.**

A: Did you just cut raw meat on that cutting board?

B: Yes, I did. Why?

A: Just make sure you wash that knife and cutting board in hot soapy water before you start cutting those vegetables.

B: How come? I'm just going to have to wash them again later.

A: I know, but that's the rule. There's a lot of dangerous bacteria in raw meat. We don't want someone to get food poisoning because we weren't careful.

B: I didn't realize that. Is there anything else I should know?

A: Yes. Remember that if customers order their beef rare, you need to explain to them that our policy is all red meat must be well done. No exceptions.

B: Got it. Thanks for telling me.

Now write True or False.

1. You need to wash things that touch raw meat. _____

2. Vegetables shouldn't be served raw. _____

3. Raw and undercooked meat may make you sick. _____

4. Customers can have their beef prepared any way they want. _____

13 Complete the sentences in the questionnaire. Use the words in the box.

before	clean	sponges	hot	refrigerator
color	after	red	cooked	bag

Is your food safe?

Fill out this food safety checklist and find out!

yes   no

1. I never buy dented cans or frozen food that isn't frozen solid.

2. I wash my hands in hot soapy water _____ I prepare food and _____ I use the bathroom or handle raw meat.

3. I never make any recipes with raw eggs in them. I don't eat food with eggs in it before it is _____.

4. I freeze fresh meat, poultry, or fish immediately if I can't use it within a couple of days.

5. I don't use food that has a strange _____ or bad smell.

6. The temperature inside my _____ is 40°F and the temperature inside my freezer is 0°F.

7. When meat is frozen, I let it thaw in the refrigerator, not on the kitchen counter.

8. I clean my cutting board and knife with _____ soapy water after I cut meat, poultry, or fish.

9. I always cook _____ meat to 160°F, and poultry to 180°F.

10. I use _____ dishes and utensils to serve food. I never use the same ones I used to prepare the food.

11. I make sure food is completely cooked before I serve or eat it.

12. After a meal, I never leave food out of the refrigerator for more than two hours.

13. When my family takes perishable food out of the house, we put it in an insulated _____ with a cold pack.

14. I wash kitchen towels often, and disinfect _____ by putting them in the microwave.

> Count up your 'yes' answers. Write the total here: _____
> *If your total is 0-11, you've got work to do! Do it now, for your health's sake!
> *If your total is 12-13, you almost have a safe kitchen. Make those important changes now!
> *If your total is 14, congratulations! Your kitchen is safe and sound!

14 Now complete the questionnaire for <u>yourself</u> and check your score.

Read the article about over-the-counter medications.

Educate yourself about OTCs
by Bonnie Crain, M.D.

Who's never had a cold? Where's the baby who hasn't suffered from teething woes, or the adult who hasn't had <u>sore</u> muscles or a headache, or an itchy rash from a food allergy?

No one gets through life without a little pain and suffering, not bad or <u>serious</u> enough to visit the doctor, but bad enough to seek relief on the pharmacy shelf.

What are OTCs?

Over-the-counter medicines, referred to as "OTCs," are medicines you can purchase without a doctor's prescription, simply by going to the nearest drugstore and choosing them yourself. Many of us make our choices based on <u>word of mouth</u>, advertisements, or by reading medicine package labels. Thousands of drugs are available over the counter, and it's important to be careful when choosing or taking them. Here are some important facts about OTCs:

1. OTCs are drugs. Just because they are available without a prescription doesn't mean they're <u>harmless</u>.
2. Many OTCs have side effects.
3. Mixing medications may be dangerous. Many OTCs can interact or interfere with the effects of your prescription drugs or with other OTCs.

How to use OTCs safely

Read package labels carefully. Be sure you understand warnings. Don't <u>exceed</u> the recommended dosage. <u>When in doubt</u>, ask the pharmacist or your doctor for advice. It's your responsibility, but the druggist and the doctor can help.

Now read the sentences. Check ☑ <u>True</u> or <u>False</u>.

	True	False
1. You need a prescription to buy OTC medications.	☐	☐
2. OTCs can be purchased at a drugstore.	☐	☐
3. It's important to read the package labels.	☐	☐
4. All OTCs are harmless and have no side effects.	☐	☐
5. It can be dangerous to take a lot of different medications at once.	☐	☐
6. You should ask for help if you don't understand the warnings on the label.	☐	☐

16 Look at the underlined words in the article. Match the underlined word(s) with its meaning. Write the letter on the line.

1. sore _____   a. take more than
2. serious _____   b. what our friends say
3. word of mouth _____   c. if you don't know
4. harmless _____   d. aching
5. exceed _____   e. completely safe
6. when in doubt _____   f. important

17 **Answer the questions about <u>yourself</u>.**

1. What kinds of OTCs do you buy? _____

2. Who can you talk to if you have questions about an OTC? _____

_____

18 ▶*CHALLENGE* **Read about Malik Johnson.**

Malik has been sick. His doctor has prescribed several different medications. Malik has a hard time remembering when to take each medication. This morning, Malik's wife bought a pill case to help her husband remember when to take his medicines.

Now read the list of medications Malik takes. For each time compartment on the pill case, write which pills he should take. Malik usually has breakfast at 10 a.m., lunch at 2 p.m., and dinner at 8 p.m.

```
Aplex         Take 1 tablet before breakfast
Nox           Take 1 daily at bedtime
Prilex        Take 3 times a day with meals
Epicillin     1 in the morning and 1 in the evening, with food
Mednizone     Take 2 caplets, 3 x day on an empty stomach at
              least 2 hours before meals
```

8 a.m. 2 Mednizone	**10 a.m.**	**noon**	**2 p.m.**
4 p.m.	**6 p.m.**	**8 p.m.**	**10 p.m.**

UNIT 9

Your money

➤ Practical conversations

1 ➤**VOCABULARY** Read the sentences. Is the news good or bad? Check ☑ the answer.

	Good news	Bad news
1. They approved my credit card application.	❏	❏
2. Your check bounced.	❏	❏
3. You're going to have to pay a penalty.	❏	❏
4. Interest rates on loans are really low right now.	❏	❏
5. They didn't approve our loan application.	❏	❏
6. There's no late fee.	❏	❏
7. My application for a car loan wasn't approved.	❏	❏
8. We've finished paying the mortgage. The house is ours!	❏	❏

2 Complete the conversations. Use the words from the box.

brochure	interest rate	right	around	application	buy

A: I'm looking for some information on loans. Are you the _____ person?

1.

B: Yes, I am. I'm Mr. Gergis. How can I help you?

A: I want to _____ a car. Can you tell me the current _____

2.   3.
on car loans?

B: As of this morning, it's 8%. Would you like to fill out an _____?

4.

A: Well, I'm still shopping _____ right now, but I'll take a _____.

5.   6.

B: Sure. Here you go.

3 **➤VOCABULARY** Look at the underlined words. Match each underlined word with its meaning. Write the letter on the line.

1. Are you <u>satisfied</u> with your current interest rate? _____   **a.** had enough

2. She's afraid they'll <u>repossess</u> her car. _____   **b.** lower

3. Is this your <u>current</u> address? _____   **c.** pleased

4. What are these <u>fees</u> for? _____   **d.** stop

5. I might need to <u>reduce</u> my payments. _____   **e.** take back

6. If you get too far behind, they could <u>cancel</u> your card. _____   **f.** charges

7. I've <u>had it</u>! _____   **g.** present

4 Complete the conversations. Use your <u>own</u> words.

1. **A:** I got some _____ news today.

   B: Really? What is it?

   A: The bank _____

   _____.

   B: _____

   _____.

2. **A:** Have you ever been behind on your

   _____?

   B: Yes, once. Why? What happened?

   A: Oh, I got in over my head, and now they might _____.

   B: I'm sorry to hear that. How far behind are you?

   A: _____.

   B: Well, if I were you, I'd _____.

   A: Maybe you're right.

➤ Practical grammar

5 Complete each unreal conditional sentence.

1. If I _____*needed*_____ a loan, I `*d shop*_____ around.

   (need)   (shop)

2. I _____ a house tomorrow if I _____ find the

   (buy)   (can)

   right house.

3. If my bank _____ the branch in my neighborhood,

   (close)

   I _____ change banks.

   (have to)

4. We _____ in debt if we _____ four credit cards.

   (not be)   (not have)

5. If you _____ me, _____ you

   (be)

   _____ your money in a savings account or a CD?

   (put)

6. If I _____ in over my head, I _____ a second job.

   (get)   (get)

6 Read the sentences. Then rewrite them as one unreal conditional sentence.

1. I don't bank at Money Tree. I don't have free checking.

   If I banked at Money Tree, I'd have free checking.

2. I don't have children. I don't buy the larger package.

   _____

3. We don't use a credit card. We aren't in debt.

   _____

4. Our bank doesn't raise its fees. We don't go to another bank.

   _____

5. They don't own a house. They don't have a mortgage.

   _____

7 ➤ CHALLENGE **Read the paragraph. Complete each unreal conditional sentence.**

Ernesto lives in an apartment in Lawson with his wife. He works downtown. Ernesto doesn't have a car, so he usually takes the bus to work. It takes forty-five minutes to get downtown by bus, but only takes twenty minutes to drive. Ernesto works part-time because he goes to school at night. He wants to finish school so he can get a full-time job that pays more money. One day Ernesto would like to buy a big house so he and his wife can start having children.

1. If Ernesto had a car, _he'd drive to work_____.

2. If Ernesto lived downtown, _____.

3. If Ernesto finished school, _____.

4. If Ernesto worked full-time, _____.

5. If Ernesto and his wife had a big house, _____.

8 **Complete each sentence about continuing actions with <u>keep</u> and gerunds. Use the verbs in the box.**

close	lower	forget	spend
spoil	call	get	~~shop around~~

1. I don't really like their rates. I think I'll _keep shopping around_ .

2. I've had it! I _____ these credit card applications in the mail.

3. If you _____ to pay that bill, we're going to have to pay a finance charge.

4. The company _____ the price of their computers. We should buy one.

5. The library _____. Are your books overdue?

6. The milk _____ before I can drink it. Maybe I should buy smaller cartons.

7. The bank must be in trouble. They _____ branches.

8. They _____ more money then they make. No wonder they're in debt!

➤ Authentic practice

9 **Read. Choose your response. Fill in the ovals.**

1. "I was living beyond my means and got into debt."

   ⓐ Where do you live? ⓑ How did that happen?

2. "First, the good news."

   ⓐ Uh-oh. That means there's bad news too. ⓑ Let's take the good news.

3. "What would you do if you were in my shoes?"

   ⓐ I'd talk to a credit counselor. ⓑ I'll shop around.

4. "This is totally ridiculous! I've had it!"

   ⓐ What do you have? ⓑ What's wrong?

5. "This might be a silly question, but what's wrong with using a credit card?"

   ⓐ It keeps you from spending more than you have. ⓑ Well, you can really get into debt.

10 **Read the conversation. Then check ☑ T (True), F (False), or ? (I don't know).**

Carla: Are you going away for vacation this summer, Dora?
Dora: I'd love to, but I'm not sure I should.
Carla: How come?
Dora: Well, I've been using my credit card a lot lately. I really need to pay down the balance of my bill before I get into any more debt.
Carla: I know what you mean. If using my credit card wasn't so convenient, I would cut it up and throw it away!
Dora: Someday I might need a loan or a mortgage, and I don't want to be turned down because of too much credit card debt. I guess I'll be spending my vacation at home this year.
Carla: Me too.

	T	F	?
1. Dora is in debt.	☐	☐	☐
2. Dora's friend, Carla, is in debt too.	☐	☐	☐
3. Dora needs a mortgage right now.	☐	☐	☐
4. Carla cut up her credit card.	☐	☐	☐
5. Neither woman will be going on vacation this summer.	☐	☐	☐

11 **Read the information about debt.**

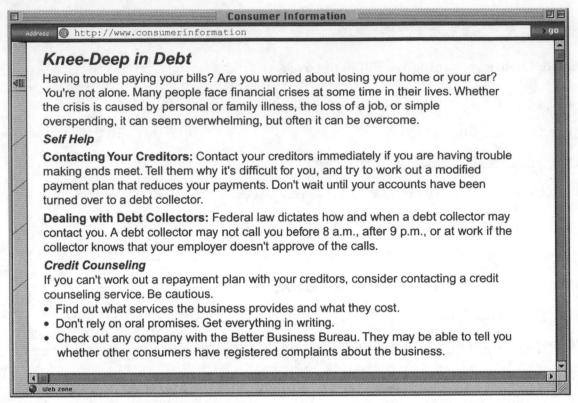

Now choose the best conclusion to each sentence. Circle the letter.

1. Most people _____.

   a. don't overspend

   b. can get out of debt

   c. can't get out of debt

2. The first thing you should do if you are getting too far into debt is _____.

   a. call a debt collector

   b. check with the Better Business Bureau

   c. talk to your creditors

3. It's illegal for a debt collector to _____.

   a. call you between 8 a.m. and 9 p.m.

   b. call you at home

   c. call you between 9 p.m. and 8 a.m.

4. Before you use a credit counseling service, you should _____.

   a. complain to the Better Business Bureau

   b. get a written description of their services and costs

   c. keep raising your payments to your creditors

12 **What's your advice? Tell these people what to do.**

1. "My husband is very sick and has been out of work for three months. We're having trouble paying our bills. What should we do?"

    YOU _____

2. "Why should I talk to the Better Business Bureau before I use a credit counseling service?"

    YOU _____

3. "A debt collector keeps calling me at work. My boss is getting mad because we're not supposed to get personal calls at work. What should I do?"

    YOU _____

13 **What would you do? Look at the situations and possible solutions. Write sentences. Use the words in the columns or your own ideas.**

Problems	Possible Solutions
You are three months behind on your rent/mortgage/car payment.	ask a friend/co-worker for help
	get a loan
You are one month behind on your rent/ mortgage/car payment.	use a credit counseling service
	ask a family member for help
You have $500 in credit card debt.	stop using my credit card
You have $5,000 in credit card debt.	ask for a raise at work
You want to buy a house/ car.	start saving money
	get a second job

1. *If I was one month behind on my rent, I'd ask a friend for help*.

2. _____.

3. _____.

4. _____.

5. _____.

14 Read the bill. Then look at the answers. Write the questions.

Statement of Personal Card Account

Payable upon receipt in U.S. Dollars with a check drawn on a bank located in the U.S., or a money order.
Please enter Personal Account Number on all checks and correspondence.

C E Credit Express

YOUR ACCOUNT IS 30 DAYS PAST DUE.
PAY BY 05/18/03 TO AVOID DELINQUENCY CHARGE.

Personal Account Number	Statement Closing Date	Total Amount Due
7819 622 4700	04–26–03	**$157.18**

Roseanne Calderon
420 W. 95th St.
New York, NY 10025

Mail payment to:
Credit Express
P.O. Box 6700
Newark, NJ 07101–1270

8525924869 00097318000092257B

Detach here and return upper portion with check or money order. Do not staple or fold.

1. Whose bill is this?_____

2. How far behind is her account?_____

3. What is the total amount due? _____

4. When is the payment due? _____

5. How should she pay the bill?_____

   _____

15 Now write a check for the full amount that is past due. Use May 11, 2003 as the date.

Roseanne Calderon
420 W. 95th St.
New York, NY 10025

304

DATE_____

PAY TO THE
ORDER OF _____ $ _____

_____ **DOLLARS**

Money Tree Bank
512 E. 44 St.
New York, NY 10017

MEMO _____

Roseanne Calderon

1:041000689:1 6066066B' 304

UNIT 10

Your career

➤ Practical conversations

1 **➤VOCABULARY** **Complete the sentences. Use words from the box.**

hands-on	leave	conflict	references
moved	salary	call	opportunities

1. My company _____ to a new location so I have to find a new job.

2. Why did you decide to _____ your previous job?

3. My new job gives me a lot of _____ experience.

4. Could you send me a list of your _____?

5. Jim left his last job because there were no _____ to advance.

6. Chloe has a personality _____ with her co-worker.

7. Did the interviewer ask you about your _____ requirements?

8. My name is Marina Santos. Please _____ me Marina.

2 **Complete the conversation. Write the letter on the line.**

A: How did you hear about this job?

B: _____
   1.

A: That's great. Now, who was your last employer?

B: _____
   2.

A: And why did you leave that job?

B: _____
   3.

A: I see. What hours would you like to work?

B: _____
   4.

A: OK. Do you have any references?

B: _____
   5.

A: That's fine.

a. I need to work in the morning because I go to school at night.

b. I saw your ad at the employment center.

c. Of course. May I send you a list tomorrow?

d. Well, I worked at a restaurant in Newcastle for two years.

e. I liked the job, but the hours weren't good for me.

3 Complete the chart. Use your <u>own</u> words.

Things you like about your job	Things you don't like about your job

4 Complete the conversations. Use your <u>own</u> words.

A: Well, _____, you've had a

_____ with us.

You're really doing a _____

job.

B: Thank you, Ms. _____.

I'm _____.

A: _____ call me _____. Everyone else does.

B: _____.

A: Now, I've been meaning to ask you about where you see yourself in _____.

B: Well, I think I'd like to be _____, but I'm not sure. Are there any

opportunities for _____?

A: Absolutely.

5 Answer the questions about yourself.

1. Who are you on a first-name basis with at work? _____

2. Who are you <u>not</u> on a first-name basis with at work? _____

3. Where do you see yourself three years from now? _____

_____

4. What was the reason you left your last job? _____

_____

➤ Practical grammar

6 Complete each sentence with the simple present tense or the present continuous.

1. Employees like Nola because she ____*praises*____ them when they do a good job.

praise

2. Hey, Franco! It's 5:30. I _____ now!

leave

3. Why do you _____ to change jobs?

want

4. The home office is in Portland. I _____ my hours to them

fax

every week.

5. I haven't seen you in ages! What _____ you _____

do

these days?

6. In my country, employees usually _____ supervisors by their

not call

first names.

7. How often do you _____ performance reviews in your company?

have

8. Sarah can't come to lunch with us. She _____ to her supervisor

talk

right now.

7 Read the questions. Then write an answer for each sentence. Use the present perfect or the present perfect continuous.

1. **A:** How long have they been fixing cars?

   B: *They've been fixing cars since 1988.* _____

2. **A:** How long has Aisha worked here?

   B: _____

3. **A:** How long have we studied English?

   B: _____

4. **A:** How long have you been living at that address?

   B: _____

5. **A:** How long has Aldo been taking care of children?

   B: _____

8 ►CHALLENGE Look at the time line for Andrew Chow. Then complete the sentences about his life. Use the present perfect or the present perfect continuous.

came to U.S.	got first job	started studying English	moved to Dover	left first job & got a job at Delaney's Nursery	promoted to supervisor
March 1998	May 1998	Sept. 1998	Dec. 1999	Feb. 2000	May 2002

1. Andrew Chow _____ in the United States for _____.

2. He _____ at Delaney's Nursery for _____.

3. Mr. Chow _____ in Dover for _____.

4. He _____ English since _____.

5. He _____ as a supervisor since _____.

9 Make a time line about your life. Then write sentences about yourself using your time line.

1. I've _____

2. I've _____

3. I've _____

4. I've _____

➤ Authentic practice

🔟 Read. Choose your response. Fill in the ovals.

1. "Do you have a second?"

   ⓐ Sure. What's up?   ⓑ Yes. I'm happy to hear that.

2. "I think it's time we talked about getting you some management training."

   ⓐ I am? Thanks.   ⓑ Really? Thanks.

3. "I've been hearing some terrific things about you."

   ⓐ Thanks. I've been working hard.   ⓑ Has there been a problem?

4. "Let them know that you appreciate the work they're doing."

   ⓐ I'll try that. Thanks for the input. ⓑ I can give you a list.

5. "I've been meaning to talk to her about her people skills."

   ⓐ You're doing a great job.   ⓑ Why don't you do that at the performance review?

⓫ Read the conversation. Then answer the questions.

Lisa: How did your performance review go?
Fred: Pretty good. My boss said he's been hearing great things about me.
Lisa: Really? Well, that's good news.
Fred: Yeah, but there was one thing that wasn't so good.
Lisa: What's that?
Fred: Well, he thinks some of my workers don't feel like I appreciate them.
Lisa: Did he suggest what you could do to make things better?
Fred: He suggested I check in with them more often to see how things are going and to praise them for doing such a great job.
Lisa: That's good advice. A little praise can make all the difference in the world.
Fred: You're right. I'm going to try to be more supportive of my workers from now on.

1. What is Fred telling Lisa about? _____

   _____

2. Why are Fred's workers unhappy? _____

   _____

3. What did Fred's boss suggest he do to make the workers feel better?

   _____

12 **Read the sentences. Then choose the word or phrase that is the closest in meaning to the underlined word(s). Circle the letter.**

1. My boss saw me in the office after 5:00 and he said, "Andy! Go home. <u>Get out of here!</u> You've done enough for today."

   a. go outside   **b.** get a new job   **c.** leave for the day

2. Our supervisor showed us he <u>recognized</u> all our hard work by giving us a raise.

   a. was aware of   **b.** forgot   **c.** required

3. Monica told me how much she appreciates your <u>effort</u>.

   a. opportunity   **b.** hard work   **c.** hours

4. In this country, it is <u>normal</u> to joke around with your co-workers.

   a. extra   **b.** something everyone does   **c.** hands-on

5. We're <u>looking forward</u> to having you work with us for a long time.

   a. watching   **b.** hoping   **c.** worrying

13 **Read the performance review.**

Annual Performance Evaluation

Anika Marstens	Shipping Clerk	Henry Yi
Employee Name	Title	Supervisor

Shipping Department	2/8/02	2/8/02 - 2/7/03
Work Location	Hiring Date	Period of evaluation

Areas	Excellent	Satisfactory	Needs Improvement	Unsatisfactory
1. Performs job duties	☑	☐	☐	☐
2. Works well with others	☐	☑	☐	☐
3. Attendance	☑	☐	☐	☐
4. Punctuality	☑	☐	☐	☐
5. Shows initiative; makes suggestions	☐	☐	☑	☐

Is this employee recommended for a raise in salary?   ☑ yes   ☐ no

Comments: Anika has had a good first year in the shipping department. She gets along well with her co-workers but is very quiet and sometimes hesitates to offer opinions or ideas. We hope that she will become a strong "team player" in the next year.

Now read the sentences. Check ✓ True or False.

		True	False
1.	Anika works in the manufacturing department.	☐	☐
2.	She started working at the company in 2002.	☐	☐
3.	Anika comes to work on time.	☐	☐
4.	She makes lots of suggestions to her co-workers.	☐	☐
5.	Anika misses work regularly.	☐	☐
6.	She will probably get a raise this year.	☐	☐

14 **Read the want ads. Then answer the questions.**

1. Where are all these jobs located?

   a. Canton.   **b.** Private home.

2. What should you do if you want to interview for these jobs?

   a. Write a complaint letter about the ad.   **b.** Call the person named in the ad.

3. Is experience required for the counter help and personal care assistant positions?

   a. Yes.   **b.** No.

4. What do you have to do if you want to apply for the driver job?

   a. Speak fluent English.   **b.** Fax your job history and driving record.

5. If you were looking for a job, which one would you apply for? Why?

   _____

   _____

15 ➤ CHALLENGE **Call about one of the ads in Exercise 14. Use your <u>own</u> name and words.**

Interviewer: Hello?

YOU Hi, my name is _____. I'm calling in

response to your ad for a _____ in today's

paper. Is this _____?

Interviewer: Yes, it is. Can I ask you a few questions?

YOU _____

Interviewer: Do you have any experience with this type of work?

YOU _____

Interviewer: OK. Now, what was your last job?

YOU _____

Interviewer: And why did you leave that position?

YOU _____

Interviewer: Do you have any other skills you'd like to tell me about?

YOU _____

Interviewer: Are you working now?

YOU _____

Interviewer: OK. When are you available to come in for an interview?

YOU _____

Interviewer: That would be fine. I'll look forward to seeing you then.

YOU _____

Skills for test taking

Write your information in the boxes. Fill in the ovals.

LAST NAME															FIRST NAME															MI
A	A	A	A	A	A	A	A	A	A	A	A	A	A	A	A	A	A	A	A	A	A	A	A	A	A	A	A	A	A	A
B	B	B	B	B	B	B	B	B	B	B	B	B	B	B	B	B	B	B	B	B	B	B	B	B	B	B	B	B	B	B
C	C	C	C	C	C	C	C	C	C	C	C	C	C	C	C	C	C	C	C	C	C	C	C	C	C	C	C	C	C	C
D	D	D	D	D	D	D	D	D	D	D	D	D	D	D	D	D	D	D	D	D	D	D	D	D	D	D	D	D	D	D
E	E	E	E	E	E	E	E	E	E	E	E	E	E	E	E	E	E	E	E	E	E	E	E	E	E	E	E	E	E	E
F	F	F	F	F	F	F	F	F	F	F	F	F	F	F	F	F	F	F	F	F	F	F	F	F	F	F	F	F	F	F
G	G	G	G	G	G	G	G	G	G	G	G	G	G	G	G	G	G	G	G	G	G	G	G	G	G	G	G	G	G	G
H	H	H	H	H	H	H	H	H	H	H	H	H	H	H	H	H	H	H	H	H	H	H	H	H	H	H	H	H	H	H
I	I	I	I	I	I	I	I	I	I	I	I	I	I	I	I	I	I	I	I	I	I	I	I	I	I	I	I	I	I	I
J	J	J	J	J	J	J	J	J	J	J	J	J	J	J	J	J	J	J	J	J	J	J	J	J	J	J	J	J	J	J
K	K	K	K	K	K	K	K	K	K	K	K	K	K	K	K	K	K	K	K	K	K	K	K	K	K	K	K	K	K	K
L	L	L	L	L	L	L	L	L	L	L	L	L	L	L	L	L	L	L	L	L	L	L	L	L	L	L	L	L	L	L
M	M	M	M	M	M	M	M	M	M	M	M	M	M	M	M	M	M	M	M	M	M	M	M	M	M	M	M	M	M	M
N	N	N	N	N	N	N	N	N	N	N	N	N	N	N	N	N	N	N	N	N	N	N	N	N	N	N	N	N	N	N
O	O	O	O	O	O	O	O	O	O	O	O	O	O	O	O	O	O	O	O	O	O	O	O	O	O	O	O	O	O	O
P	P	P	P	P	P	P	P	P	P	P	P	P	P	P	P	P	P	P	P	P	P	P	P	P	P	P	P	P	P	P
Q	Q	Q	Q	Q	Q	Q	Q	Q	Q	Q	Q	Q	Q	Q	Q	Q	Q	Q	Q	Q	Q	Q	Q	Q	Q	Q	Q	Q	Q	Q
R	R	R	R	R	R	R	R	R	R	R	R	R	R	R	R	R	R	R	R	R	R	R	R	R	R	R	R	R	R	R
S	S	S	S	S	S	S	S	S	S	S	S	S	S	S	S	S	S	S	S	S	S	S	S	S	S	S	S	S	S	S
T	T	T	T	T	T	T	T	T	T	T	T	T	T	T	T	T	T	T	T	T	T	T	T	T	T	T	T	T	T	T
U	U	U	U	U	U	U	U	U	U	U	U	U	U	U	U	U	U	U	U	U	U	U	U	U	U	U	U	U	U	U
V	V	V	V	V	V	V	V	V	V	V	V	V	V	V	V	V	V	V	V	V	V	V	V	V	V	V	V	V	V	V
W	W	W	W	W	W	W	W	W	W	W	W	W	W	W	W	W	W	W	W	W	W	W	W	W	W	W	W	W	W	W
X	X	X	X	X	X	X	X	X	X	X	X	X	X	X	X	X	X	X	X	X	X	X	X	X	X	X	X	X	X	X
Y	Y	Y	Y	Y	Y	Y	Y	Y	Y	Y	Y	Y	Y	Y	Y	Y	Y	Y	Y	Y	Y	Y	Y	Y	Y	Y	Y	Y	Y	Y
Z	Z	Z	Z	Z	Z	Z	Z	Z	Z	Z	Z	Z	Z	Z	Z	Z	Z	Z	Z	Z	Z	Z	Z	Z	Z	Z	Z	Z	Z	Z

DATE OF BIRTH		
Month	Day	Year 19__
Jan	0 0	0 0
Feb	1 1	1 1
Mar	2 2	2 2
Apr	3 3	3 3
May	4	4 4
Jun	5	5 5
Jul	6	6 6
Aug	7	7 7
Sep	8	8 8
Oct	9	9 9
Nov		
Dec		

TELEPHONE NUMBER									
0	0	0	0	0	0	0	0	0	0
1	1	1	1	1	1	1	1	1	1
2	2	2	2	2	2	2	2	2	2
3	3	3	3	3	3	3	3	3	3
4	4	4	4	4	4	4	4	4	4
5	5	5	5	5	5	5	5	5	5
6	6	6	6	6	6	6	6	6	6
7	7	7	7	7	7	7	7	7	7
8	8	8	8	8	8	8	8	8	8
9	9	9	9	9	9	9	9	9	9

TODAY'S DATE		
Month	Day	Year 20__
Jan	0 0	0 0
Feb	1 1	1 1
Mar	2 2	2 2
Apr	3 3	3
May	4	4
Jun	5	5
Jul	6	6
Aug	7	7
Sep	8	8
Oct	9	9
Nov		
Dec		

Unit 1

Choose an answer.

| Loyola Long-Term Care Center | PRE-EMPLOYMENT APPLICATION |

Loyola Long-Term Care Center
1600 Oak Crest
Belmont, CA 94128
Date of application: _____ *6/29/03*

Cheri Montagne
Applicant's name

354 North Beach, Apt. 211, Belmont, CA 94128
Current mailing address

Are you currently employed? [circle one] (Y)/ N   If yes, position: _____ *Hotel housekeeper*
Employer and address: *Motel 24, 19830 Richdale Highway, Belmont*
How long have you been working for this employer? *1 year*
If not currently employed, last position held: _____
Dates: from _____ to _____
Describe the type of position you are seeking: *Nurse's aide*
_____

Please list your skills (Examples: **driving, repairing equipment, speaking another language, etc.**).
working with people, speaking French, cleaning

1. Where does Ms. Montagne currently work?

   A. At Motel 24.
   B. At Loyola Long-Term Care Center.
   C. On North Beach Street.
   D. We don't know.

2. What is one of Ms. Montagne's skills?

   A. Driving.
   B. Repairing equipment.
   C. Using a computer.
   D. Speaking another language.

3. What job is Ms. Montagne applying for?

   A. Housekeeper.
   B. Nurse's aide.
   C. French teacher.
   D. Supervisor.

1. Ⓐ Ⓑ Ⓒ Ⓓ

2. Ⓐ Ⓑ Ⓒ Ⓓ

3. Ⓐ Ⓑ Ⓒ Ⓓ

To Whom It May Concern:

   Mr. Takamura has been working at the Briar School for three years. He is one of the best lab technicians we have and is always on time. Mr. Takamura repairs the computers and helps students in the computer classes. He enjoys fixing problems and working with students, and he doesn't mind staying late when someone needs extra help. I can recommend Mr. Takamura for a job with your company.

Sincerely,

Brenda Oliver

Brenda Oliver
Director

4. A. Ms. Oliver filled out an application.
   B. Ms. Oliver wrote a letter of recommendation.
   C. Mr. Takamura wrote a letter of recommendation.
   D. Ms. Oliver wrote a letter to a friend.

5. A. Mr. Takamura doesn't like working with students.
   B. Ms. Oliver dislikes Mr. Takamura.
   C. Mr. Takamura likes fixing problems.
   D. Mr. Takamura can't stand working late.

4. Ⓐ Ⓑ Ⓒ Ⓓ

5. Ⓐ Ⓑ Ⓒ Ⓓ

Unit 2

Choose an answer.

Open House!

Please come to our first party in our new house!

Date: 8/2/03

Time: 3 p.m. - 7 p.m.

Place: 493 Spring Lake Road, Newton

RSVP: 555-9188

Spring Lake Road is between Madison Street and Route 7.
Please call if you need directions.

Hope you can come!   Joy and Omar Lawson

1. Where is the Lawsons' house?

   A. On Madison Street.
   B. Between Madison Street and Spring Lake Road.
   C. At the corner of Madison Street and Route 7.
   D. On Spring Lake Road.

2. What time should you arrive at the party?

   A. On August 2.
   B. On February 3.
   C. At 3:00 p.m.
   D. At 7:00 p.m.

1. Ⓐ Ⓑ Ⓒ Ⓓ

2. Ⓐ Ⓑ Ⓒ Ⓓ

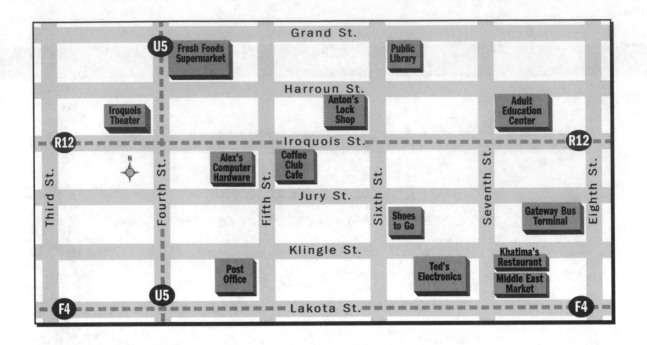

3. Alex's Computer Hardware store is
   _____.

   A. next to the Coffee Club Cafe
   B. at the corner of Fourth and
      Iroquois
   C. across from the Coffee Club Cafe
   D. on Harroun Street

4. _____ is at the corner of
   Sixth and Klingle.

   A. Shoes to Go
   B. The F4 bus
   C. Khatima's Restaurant
   D. Ted's Electronics

5. Start at the corner of Fourth and
   Lakota. Take the U5 bus to Iroquois
   Street. Transfer there to the R12 bus.
   Get off at Seventh Street. You are
   _____.

   A. at the Middle East Market
   B. across from the Public Library
   C. at the Adult Education Center
   D. between Jury Street and Klingle
      Street

3. Ⓐ Ⓑ Ⓒ Ⓓ

4. Ⓐ Ⓑ Ⓒ Ⓓ

5. Ⓐ Ⓑ Ⓒ Ⓓ

Unit 3

Choose an answer.

Repair Record for ___Commercial Vacuum model 78MR31___

Date purchased __1/7/99__

Date Serviced	Service	Technician's Name
8/15/99	cleaned	T.S. Reed
8/15/00	cleaned	T.S. Reed
1/29/01	main hose replaced	T.S. Reed
8/20/01	cleaned	Paula Vladic
8/2/02	belts replaced	Paula Vladic
8/2/02	cleaned	Otis Sayres
8/27/03	cleaned	B.A. Vo

1. A. The vacuum was cleaned once a year.
   B. The vacuum wasn't cleaned in 2001.
   C. The vacuum was purchased in 1997.
   D. The vacuum was replaced in 2002.

2. A. The vacuum is always serviced by the same technician.
   B. T. S. Reed cleaned the vacuum three times.
   C. The vacuum was cleaned by Paula Vladic two years after it was purchased.
   D. The vacuum was repaired by B.A. Vo in 2002 and 2003.

1. Ⓐ Ⓑ Ⓒ Ⓓ

2. Ⓐ Ⓑ Ⓒ Ⓓ

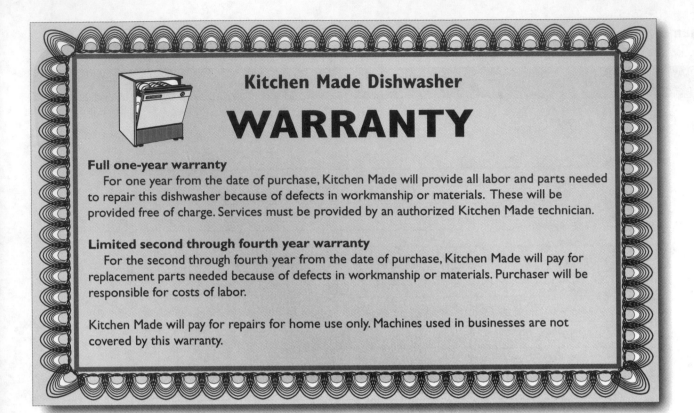

Kitchen Made Dishwasher

WARRANTY

Full one-year warranty

For one year from the date of purchase, Kitchen Made will provide all labor and parts needed to repair this dishwasher because of defects in workmanship or materials. These will be provided free of charge. Services must be provided by an authorized Kitchen Made technician.

Limited second through fourth year warranty

For the second through fourth year from the date of purchase, Kitchen Made will pay for replacement parts needed because of defects in workmanship or materials. Purchaser will be responsible for costs of labor.

Kitchen Made will pay for repairs for home use only. Machines used in businesses are not covered by this warranty.

3. What does the warranty cover during the first year?

   A. Parts only.
   B. Parts and labor.
   C. Labor only.
   D. Service by any technician.

4. What is covered by the warranty in the third year?

   A. Parts only.
   B. Parts and labor.
   C. Labor only.
   D. Purchase of a new dishwasher.

5. Which statement is true about this dishwasher?

   A. It is under warranty for one year if it is used in a restaurant.
   B. It is under warranty for four years if it is used in a restaurant.
   C. It is not under warranty if it is used in a home.
   D. It is not under warranty if it is used in a restaurant.

3. Ⓐ Ⓑ Ⓒ Ⓓ

4. Ⓐ Ⓑ Ⓒ Ⓓ

5. Ⓐ Ⓑ Ⓒ Ⓓ

Unit 4

Choose an answer.

> Dear Sir or Madam:
>
> I am writing to complain about Bleach-O, which is made by your company. The cleaner is great. We use it all the time and it cleans our kitchen and bathroom really well. I used to buy another cleaner, but Bleach-O is much better.
>
> However, I am dissastisfied with the plastic container Bleach-O comes in. It's terrible! I have bought three containers of Bleach-O in the last year, and all of them have broken. Please let me know if Bleach-O is sold in any other container. This one is no good!
>
> Sincerely,
> Marta Berlioz

1. What is Ms. Berlioz's problem with Bleach-O?

   A.   The cleaner is fantastic.
   B.   The cleaner is no good.
   C.   The containers are not clean.
   D.   The containers are not good.

2. What does Ms. Berlioz want?

   A.   She wants to buy Bleach-O in a better container.
   B.   She wants a refund.
   C.   She wants Bleach-O to be recalled.
   D.   She wants to use the cleaner she used to buy.

1.   Ⓐ Ⓑ Ⓒ Ⓓ

2.   Ⓐ Ⓑ Ⓒ Ⓓ

Curbside Recycling Policy

- Your curbside recycling day is Thursday.
- Please put glass (clear, green or brown), plastic bottles and containers, and metal cans in the yellow recycling bin.
- Please put newspaper and cardboard (no food, please) in the blue bin.
- Leave the bins at the curb next to the street on Wednesday evening.
- These items should NOT be placed in your bins: used car oil, batteries, paint cans. These items can be recycled on the first Sunday of every month at Hazardous Waste Collection Day at Roosevelt High School.

Thank you for helping our community by recycling!

---

3. A. Curbside recycling is picked up on Wednesday.
    B. Curbside recycling is picked up on Thursday.
    C. Curbside recycling is picked up on Saturday.
    D. Curbside recycling is picked up on Sunday.

4. A. Car oil, batteries, and paint cans should go in the blue bin.
    B. Car oil, batteries, and paint cans should go in the yellow bin.
    C. Car oil, batteries, and paint cans should be taken to Roosevelt High School.
    D. Car oil, batteries, and paint cans cannot be recycled.

5. A. You should put a brown glass soda bottle in the blue bin.
    B. You should put a green glass bottle in the yellow bin.
    C. You should take newspapers to Roosevelt High School.
    D. You should put the bins at the curb on Friday.

3. Ⓐ Ⓑ Ⓒ Ⓓ

4. Ⓐ Ⓑ Ⓒ Ⓓ

5. Ⓐ Ⓑ Ⓒ Ⓓ

Unit 5

Choose an answer.

> **MEMO**
>
> TO: All Sunshine employees
> From: Raquel Ortiz, HR Manager
> Re: Company policy reminders
>
> We'd like to remind you of the following company
> policies:
> - All employees are expected to complete personal
>   business on their own time.
> - Company computers are not for personal use.
> - Company telephones may to used for personal
>   business only in an emergency.
>
> If you have any questions about these policies, please
> speak with your supervisor or the Human Resources
> department. Thank you for your cooperation!

1. A. This is a policy about an employer's expectations.
    B. This is a policy about being punctual.
    C. This is a policy about rescheduling events.
    D. This is a policy about emergencies.

2. A. Employees should do personal business on company time.
    B. Employees should use the company computers for personal business.
    C. Employees should do personal business on their own time.
    D. Employees should use the computers in Human Resources.

1. Ⓐ Ⓑ Ⓒ Ⓓ

2. Ⓐ Ⓑ Ⓒ Ⓓ

PARKING ATTENDANT

Minimum wage $5.15/hr. + tips
Overtime pay: time and a half
Shifts: first: 7 a.m. to 3 p.m. with
one-hour break for lunch.
second: 3 p.m. to 11 p.m. with
one-hour break for dinner.

• BEAUTICIAN'S ASSISTANT •

Pt.-time Immediate
Responsibilities: wash clients' hair.
Salary: $4.80/hr. plus tips. Hours:
Tuesdays & Wednesdays 11:00
a.m. to 4:00 p.m. Experienced only.

GARDENERS NEEDED

FT + seasonal
$6 / hr.;
Hrs: 7 a.m. – 3 p.m. M-F;
OT: Time + 1/2 on weekends
Experience preferred

3. Which jobs are paid by the hour, plus tips?

A. The parking attendant and the gardener.
B. The parking attendant and the beautician's assistant.
C. The gardener and the beautician's assistant.
D. All the jobs.

4. How many hours a week will the beautician's assistant work?

A. Eleven hours.
B. Ten hours.
C. Ten and a half hours.
D. Sixteen hours.

5. What is the overtime pay for the gardener's job?

A. $3.00 per hour.
B. $6.00 per hour.
C. $9.00 per hour.
D. $12.00 per hour.

3. Ⓐ Ⓑ Ⓒ

4. Ⓐ Ⓑ Ⓒ

5. Ⓐ Ⓑ Ⓒ

Unit 6

Choose an answer.

YOU PAY	UNIT PRICE
$2.99	**9.3¢** PER OZ.
32 oz. Sun Maid Orange Juice	‖‖‖‖ 145 918 32

YOU PAY	UNIT PRICE
$4.49	**7.0¢** PER OZ.
64 oz. Sun Maid Orange Juice	‖‖‖‖ 145 936 64

YOU PAY	UNIT PRICE
$3.99	**12.5¢** PER OZ.
32 oz. Orange Plus Orange Juice w/calcium	‖‖‖‖ 145 730 32

1. A. The 32-ounce bottle of Sun Maid Orange Juice costs 9.3 cents.
    B. The 32-ounce bottle of Sun Maid Orange Juice costs $2.99.
    C. The 32-ounce bottle of Sun Maid Orange Juice costs $3.99.
    D. The 32-ounce bottle of Sun Maid Orange Juice costs $4.49.

2. A. The 32-ounce bottle of Sun Maid is cheaper per ounce than Orange Plus.
    B. The 64-ounce bottle of Sun Maid is as expensive per ounce as Orange Plus.
    C. Orange Plus is not as expensive per ounce as the 32-ounce bottle of Sun Maid.
    D. Orange Plus is the cheapest brand of orange juice per ounce.

1. Ⓐ Ⓑ Ⓒ Ⓓ

2. Ⓐ Ⓑ Ⓒ Ⓓ

ORDER FORM

A	B	C	D	E	F
Item Description	Item number	Color	Quantity	Unit Price	Total Price

Standard Round Pencils

Lead: #2 soft unsharpened

As low as $0.19

Pencil colors: Dark blue, dark green, red, white, lemon yellow, school bus yellow, assorted light colors, assorted dark colors

Quantity	500	1000	2500	5000
Each	$0.26	$0.24	$0.22	$0.19

3. If you order 1000 red pencils, you will have to pay _____.

   A. $240.00
   B. $24.00
   C. $2.40
   D. $0.24

4. If you want to pay 19 cents for each pencil, you have to order

   _____.

   A. 500 pencils
   B. 1000 pencils
   C. 2500 pencils
   D. 5000 pencils

5. In column D of the order form, you should write _____.

   A. #2
   B. 500
   C. dark blue
   D. $0.26

3. Ⓐ Ⓑ Ⓒ Ⓓ

4. Ⓐ Ⓑ Ⓒ Ⓓ

5. Ⓐ Ⓑ Ⓒ Ⓓ

Unit 7

Choose an answer.

| Sign 1 | Sign 2 | Sign 3 | Sign 4 | Sign 5 |

1. Which sign says that you must wear a seat belt when you are driving?

   A. Sign 1.
   B. Sign 2.
   C. Sign 3.
   D. Sign 4.

2. Which sign says that it's against the law to make a U-turn on this street?

   A. Sign 5.
   B. Sign 2.
   C. Sign 1.
   D. Sign 3.

3. What does Sign 4 say?

   A. It's illegal to make a left turn.
   B. It's illegal to let your dog off the leash.
   C. It's illegal to throw trash on the street.
   D. We don't know.

1. Ⓐ Ⓑ Ⓒ Ⓓ

2. Ⓐ Ⓑ Ⓒ Ⓓ

3. Ⓐ Ⓑ Ⓒ Ⓓ

Dear Lulu,

Congratulations on the birth of Anisa's son! You must be very happy. People say that having a grandchild is wonderful. I know that will be true for you! Please tell Anisa and her husband how happy I am for them and the new baby.

Love,
Oliva

4. A. Lulu just had a baby.
    B. Oliva just had a baby.
    C. Anisa just had a baby.
    D. Oliva's daughter just had a baby.

5. A. The new baby is a girl.
    B. The new baby is Lulu's son.
    C. The new baby is Oliva's grandchild.
    D. The new baby is Lulu's grandchild.

4. Ⓐ Ⓑ Ⓒ Ⓓ

5. Ⓐ Ⓑ Ⓒ Ⓓ

Unit 8

Choose an answer.

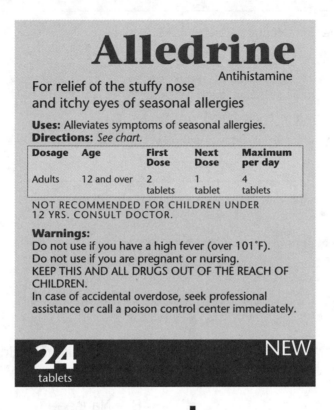

Alledrine
Antihistamine

For relief of the stuffy nose
and itchy eyes of seasonal allergies

Uses: Alleviates symptoms of seasonal allergies.
Directions: *See chart.*

Dosage	Age	First Dose	Next Dose	Maximum per day
Adults	12 and over	2 tablets	1 tablet	4 tablets

NOT RECOMMENDED FOR CHILDREN UNDER
12 YRS. CONSULT DOCTOR.

Warnings:
Do not use if you have a high fever (over 101°F).
Do not use if you are pregnant or nursing.
KEEP THIS AND ALL DRUGS OUT OF THE REACH OF
CHILDREN.
In case of accidental overdose, seek professional
assistance or call a poison control center immediately.

24 tablets

NEW

1. A. Alledrine is a medicine for a rash.
   B. Alledrine is a medicine for allergies.
   C. Alledrine is a medicine for colds.
   D. Alledrine is a medicine for a sore throat.

2. A. It's OK for everyone to take this medicine.
   B. Adults shouldn't take this medicine.
   C. Pregnant women shouldn't take this medicine.
   D. Children under 12 years should take this medicine.

1. Ⓐ Ⓑ Ⓒ Ⓓ

2. Ⓐ Ⓑ Ⓒ Ⓓ

```
Patient Instructions for: Leona Capelli
Prescribed by: Dr. Larisa Markova
Pharmacist: Suad Musa, RPh
Bactizide, 40 mg
```

Rx

Directions:	Take one capsule twice daily.
Uses:	Treats a variety of bacterial infections.
How to Use:	Take as directed by your doctor. Should be taken with food. Take all of this medication, even if you feel better.
Side Effects:	May cause drowsiness or nausea.
Missed Dose:	If you miss a dose, take it as soon as you remember.
Storage:	Store at room temperature. Do not store in the bathroom.

Keep this and all drugs out of the reach of children.

3. Who is this medicine for?

   A. Leona Capelli.
   B. Larisa Markova.
   C. Suad Musa.
   D. We don't know.

4. How many capsules should she take every day?

   A. One.
   B. Two.
   C. Four.
   D. Eight.

5. What is this medicine for?

   A. Drowsiness.
   B. Nausea.
   C. Food poisoning.
   D. Infection.

3. Ⓐ Ⓑ Ⓒ Ⓓ

4. Ⓐ Ⓑ Ⓒ Ⓓ

Unit 9

Choose an answer.

1. These ads are for _____.

   A. banks
   B. credit card companies
   C. debit card companies
   D. credit counseling services

2. You might call one of these companies _____.

   A. if you needed a credit card
   B. if you were in debt
   C. if you wanted to cancel a credit card
   D. if your bank kept raising its fees

1. Ⓐ Ⓑ Ⓒ Ⓓ

2. Ⓐ Ⓑ Ⓒ Ⓓ

Globalbank Expresscard

Account Number   6788 0001 9345 9011
Payment must be received by 1:00 p.m. local time on 11/20/03 to avoid penalties or fees.

Closing Date	Total Credit Line	Cash Advance Limit	New Balance	Available Credit Line
10/24/2003	$10,000	$4000	$487.65	$9512

Sale Date	Post Date	Reference Number	Activity Since Last Statement	Amount
	10/06	42131300	Payment THANK YOU	$200.66
9/26	9/27	HBX8943	MISSISSIPPI.COM 800-555-3222	146.23
9/29	9/29	QF90755	GREAT UNION MESA CA	87.65
10/02	10/02	35MD460	GAME CITY STA MARTA CA	119.76
10/04	10/07	9TCOX59	FLYING FOOT ELMSFORD CA	134.01

Account Summary							Amount Due	
Previous Balance	(+)Purchases & Advances	Payments	(-) Credits	(+)Finance Charge	(+) Late Charges	(=)New Balance	Minimum Due	20.00
$200.66	$487.65	$200.66				$487.65	Fees	
Make check payable to the order of Globalbank Expresscard							Past Due	

---

3. When was the payment for last month's bill received?

   A. On September 24.
   B. On September 26.
   C. On October 6.
   D. On October 24.

4. How much money did the customer spend during this billing period?

   A. $200.66
   B. $4,000
   C. $487.65
   D. $9,512

5. When would the client have to pay a late fee?

   A. If the company received the next payment on November 1 at 1 p.m.
   B. If the company received the next payment on November 15.
   C. If the company received the next payment on November 20 at 11 a.m.
   D. If the company received the next payment on November 20 at 2 p.m.

3. Ⓐ Ⓑ Ⓒ Ⓓ

4. Ⓐ Ⓑ Ⓒ Ⓓ

5. Ⓐ Ⓑ Ⓒ Ⓓ

Unit 10

Choose an answer.

— PERFORMANCE REVIEW —

Business Unit: Top Hat Clothing Company
Name: *Joao Santos*
Review Period: *2003*
Work: *Excellent work. Good people skills and very reliable.*

What are your career goals for the next few years?
I'm interested in getting some training so that I can apply for a
supervisor's position. I'm also interested in managing a store someday.

1. A. This is a job application form.
   B. This is a performance review form.
   C. This is an order form.
   D. This is a job history form.

2. A. Mr. Santos would like to be a supervisor.
   B. Mr. Santos is a supervisor.
   C. Mr. Santos would like to be a cashier.
   D. Mr. Santos is getting some training now.

1. Ⓐ Ⓑ Ⓒ Ⓓ

2. Ⓐ Ⓑ Ⓒ Ⓓ

RECEPTIONIST

For growing upscale hair salon in Fairfield. Must have good writing and communication skills. Retail exp. helpful. FT and PT available; weekdays and evenings. Fax work history to attn. of Rose Etoile, (314) 555-1400.

HOUSEKEEPING

Resthaven Retirement Home seeks a FT housekeeper, M-F, some weekends. Experience in hotel or hospital preferred. Bilingual (Spanish) preferred. Fax resume and references to Ms. Shore, (410) 555-3740. EOE

** CASHIER **

For busy auto parts store. FT only. Must be able to work Sat.-Sun. Good benefits; training provided. 555-3892; ask for Mickey.

CERTIFIED AIDE

Exp'd w/ references, will

3. If someone wants to apply for the housekeeper position, he or she should _____.

   A. go to the retirement home
   B. call Ms. Shore
   C. send a fax to Ms. Shore
   D. fill out an application

4. Angela Rubio can only work part time. She should apply for _____.

   A. the receptionist job
   B. the housekeeping job
   C. the cashier job
   D. all of the jobs

5. Working on weekends is necessary for _____.

   A. all the positions
   B. the receptionist and the cashier positions
   C. the receptionist and the housekeeping positions
   D. the cashier and the housekeeping positions

3. Ⓐ Ⓑ Ⓒ Ⓓ

4. Ⓐ Ⓑ Ⓒ Ⓓ

5. Ⓐ Ⓑ Ⓒ Ⓓ